SOUTH AFRICA
—IN THE 1980s—
STATE OF EMERGENCY

SOUTH AFRICA
──IN THE 1980s──
STATE OF EMERGENCY

First published 1980
CIIR, 22 Coleman Fields, London N1 7AF

Second edition 1983
Third edition 1986
© CIIR 1986

South Africa in the 1980s. — 3rd ed.
1. Segregation — South Africa
1. Catholic Institute for International Relations
261.7   DT763

ISBN 0 946848 39 4

Printed by the Russell Press Ltd., Bertrand Russell House, Gamble Street,
Nottingham NG7 4ET.

Photographs by Afrapix

Cover by Linda Blakemore

Contents

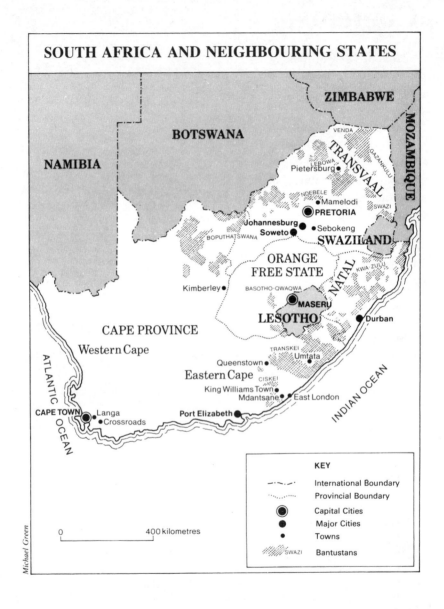

SOUTH AFRICA AND NEIGHBOURING STATES

ZIMBABWE

MOZAMBIQUE

BOTSWANA

NAMIBIA

VENDA

TRANSVAAL

GAZANKULU

LEBOWA
Pietersburg •

NDEBELE
• Mamelodi

SWAZI

⦿ PRETORIA

Johannesburg •
Soweto •
• Sebokeng

BOPUTHATSWANA

SWAZILAND

ORANGE
FREE STATE

Kimberley •

BASOTHO-QWAQWA

KWA-ZULU

NATAL

● MASERU

LESOTHO

• Durban

CAPE PROVINCE

Western Cape

TRANSKEI
• Umtata

Queenstown •

Eastern Cape

CISKEI

King Williams Town •

Mdantsane •• East London

CAPE TOWN ● • Langa
• Crossroads

Port Elizabeth •

ATLANTIC OCEAN

INDIAN OCEAN

Michael Green

KEY	
—·—·—	International Boundary
············	Provincial Boundary
⦿	Capital Cities
●	Major Cities
•	Towns
SWAZI	Bantustans

0   400 kilometres

4

Preface to the Third Edition

South Africa in the 1980s was first published in December 1980, early in the crisis that is now a permanent feature of southern Africa. It was translated into several European languages and gained a wide readership in South Africa. It provided a Christian contribution to South Africans' growing analysis of the crisis in their country by reflecting an important body of radical Christian and non-Christian opinion. A second updated edition appeared in November 1983.

It is now banned in South Africa and five critical years have elapsed to test its predictions. The evidence of these years does not demand a major rewriting of *South Africa in the 1980s*, rather updating and refinement of its earlier arguments.

Our sources have remained diverse but mainly drawn from the insights of white and black South Africans living today in the Republic. Perhaps the most important section of these sources have been South African Christians who, through the network of the universal Church, are able to present their perceptions of their society to a wide audience. By drawing together their experience into a coherent analysis for discussion, CIIR hopes to be able to establish a common framework for debate about the future of South Africa, the outstanding international problem of the decade. In this edition a number of recent documents illustrating responses to the crisis and to the state of emergency are included, together with recent photographs.

Introduction

On 21 July 1985, Mr P.W. Botha declared a state of emergency affecting about one third of South Africa's population. It was extended on 26 October to the greater Cape Town area. Nationwide, police and army personnel have been given a free rein and indemnified from any legal action.

The results were seen nightly on television screens in the West, until Pretoria imposed severe censorship on foreign correspondents and reduced foreign coverage of disorder to the low level seen in South Africa. High levels of state violence and repression also prevail in non-emergency areas where the standard Internal Security Act, rather than the new Public Safety Act, was used to detain 1,633 people in the first ten months of 1985.

The present crisis arises from a dramatic upsurge in black resistance to apartheid. Black South Africa is insisting on true democracy rather than 'reform' from above. A powerful national alliance of anti-government organisations, the United Democratic Front, was created from provincial groups at a mass meeting in Cape Town on 20 August 1983. Never since the Congress movement of the 1950s has black politics emerged nationally in a more powerful and self-confident form. Opposition led by the UDF and the trades unions to the new ethnic constitution, which created a parliament divided into chambers for whites, 'Indians' and 'coloureds', mobilised blacks to an unprecedented degree. Excluded from central government, Africans in townships throughout South Africa rejected the black local authorities offered to them as a substitute for representation in parliament. Young people took to the streets in a permanent state of insurrection.

The vast majority of the 6,000 people detained between July and November 1985 were members of the UDF and its affiliates. Over a half of the UDF's 80 office-bearers have been detained, put on trial or murdered. The township death toll touched 450 in this period. Mr P.W. Botha's claim that the state of emergency has been imposed on ten million South Africans to re-establish normal community life is clearly contradicted by events. It is there to crush democratic opposition organised in the UDF. The legal standing of these charges was shown when 12 of the 18 treason trialists at Pietermaritzburg had all charges against them dropped on 9 December 1985.

The state of emergency with its accompanying state violence was a natural progression in government policy towards its black majority. The government has always ruled by force rather than consent. But the daily killing of civilians by security forces, the banning of the Congress of South African Students (COSAS), with the detention of some 500 of its members, the arrest of young children and respected

7

community leaders, have taken South Africa to a new peak of civil disorder amounting to insurrection. Countless families and whole communities have been mobilised. Young black people today understand themselves to be engaged in a war with an army of occupation. Their perception is shared by the army and police.

At the beginning of 1983 the military wing of the African National Congress (ANC) moved from its limited campaign of sabotage to a more devastating form of urban guerrilla warfare which necessarily risked civilian casualties. Journalists' accounts of interviews with blacks after a bomb explosion outside the Pretoria headquarters of the South African airforce nonetheless reported how the majority welcomed this escalation of the war against apartheid. Three years later, after the West has become aware of the savage conduct of South African security forces towards the civilian population of black townships, this support for armed resistance should cause no surprise.

The South African government clings to its belief that state violence will permit it to ride out this unprecedented wave of rebellion. The business community, facing threats of more severe economic sanctions, and more sensitive to the consequences of prolonged instability, urgently seeks a rapid movement to something new, possibly a federal South Africa. Its trek away from the National Party has continued with the formation of a National Convention Alliance, an improbable and short-lived hybrid of the white liberal Progressive Federal Party and the Zulu movement Inkatha. Big business has struck out for the promised land, passing prudently through Lusaka for discussions with the African National Congress on the way.

The disarray indicated by these extraordinary manoeuvres may spell an early retirement from the State Presidency for Mr P.W. Botha, whose temperament and limited intelligence always made him ill-cast for the Mosaic tasks expected of him. The willingness of South African business to talk to the ANC also reveals the eccentric character of Britain's refusal to do likewise, which is inevitably seen in South Africa as a clear sign of preference for the present regime.

The championing of Inkatha and its leader Chief Buthelezi is the most thoroughly irresponsible aspect of 'third way' solutions to the South African conflict. In its home base of Natal, the repeated violence by organised gangs sometimes numbering hundreds, including attacks on church people and property, belie the non-violent image of Inkatha promoted abroad. Foreign and business support for Inkatha threatens to create an authoritarian ethnic force which could balkanise South Africa irreversibly as the collapse of the present system gains momentum. Already intimations of this disintegration in conflict over land in Kwandebele and between Zulu-speakers and Pondo, have been seen, costing many lives, as

8

apartheid-induced violence erupted at the end of 1985. The emergence of vigilante mobs and 'police' sponsored by councillors and other local apartheid authorities is not limited to Natal and represents a disturbing new phenomenon.

The spiral of violence is not contained within the borders of South Africa. The South African government appears to have concluded that its own safety depends on keeping neighbouring states not only economically dependent on South Africa but also internally divided and, if necessary, in turmoil. Weakened neighbours, it is presumed, can be no threat. The methods used have been precisely timed South African disruption of economic activity in the region, support for guerrilla and opposition movements, sabotage and direct military assault.

The impact of South Africa on neighbouring countries is very marked. Invasions and commando raids readily engender a war psychosis that has the effect of distorting social and economic priorities. Resources are shifted from urgently needed development projects to defence. In 1985, the neighbouring states in the Southern African Development Co-ordination Conference estimated that South African action had cost them US$10,000 million since 1980.

The growing power of South Africa in the region poisons race relations far beyond the Republic's border, making multi-racial cooperation fraught and brittle. Just as every black face within the Republic is treated by the government as potentially subversive, so whites in neighbouring independent states are readily, and often arbitrarily, identified as potential spies.

Western economic support for South Africa spreads the cancer of distrust into Europe and North America. Black minorities here can only view Western support for South Africa as an indication of racial bias, and as fuel to their fears in the tense conditions of economic recession. Riots in Miami, London and Cape Town are all too simply seen as part of the same process, both by blacks and by the South African government.

But the dialogue between races and minorities is not the only well poisoned by apartheid. The damage done to the North-South dialogue is perhaps equally serious. The West's position on South Africa is widely taken as a symbol of an underlying hypocrisy on the world issue of development aid and global economic stability. It is a symbol of growing importance to the Commonwealth and emotive even for those African countries obliged, of necessity, to maintain economic relations with South Africa. Serious attempts to confront the issue of South Africa would be likely to produce a significant improvement in the West's fragile relationship with the Third World.

Governments in the USA and Europe have been obliged to respond to mounting public pressure and impose limited economic sanctions against South Africa. Yet, in practice, the West still participates in the transfer of technology to South Africa and has invested heavily in its apartheid economy. It remains an accomplice in a tragedy that is unwinding with all too obvious inevitability.

It will remain the constant temptation of the West to tinker in South African solutions, 'managing change', manipulating 'reforms' and 'deals' from above. If the West is serious about the democracy it professes it must now acknowledge what is obvious: that black South Africa utterly rejects 'reform' from above without its consent. No amount of state violence will alter the fact.

Britain has a unique responsibility in this situation. Not only is a large percentage of the white South African population of British stock but Britain also bears historically the imperial responsibility for the political evolution of the Republic of South Africa in the early twentieth century. The choice between South Africa and the rest of Africa is the last one successive British governments have wanted to make. But this position has become increasingly untenable. In the short term South Africa's destabilisation of its neighbours not only threatens European investment and aid projects but also runs the risk of importing the superpower conflict as South Africa's neighbours seek defenders.

In the long run, too, Europe cannot have its cake now and eat it later, as some strategists hope. What happens in South Africa cannot be projected from previous models of decolonisation. The situation, in which a long-standing, essentially socialist-inspired, nationalist movement confronts a militarily entrenched white minority, contains the seeds of revolution, not decolonisation. Investment in South Africa is investment in the preconditions for a revolution of unprecedented proportions.

For the churches, South Africa represents a unique threat. Spokesmen for the apartheid system and those who support and enforce it frequently appeal directly to Christianity to justify their actions. Blacks, who are in practice treated merely as labour units, are presented by the government as part of a 'western Christian civilisation' which the state defends against 'communism'. Oppression and exploitation in South Africa are thus sanctioned by what amounts to blasphemy. The explanation of blacks' struggle for human rights in South Africa as a battle between 'christianity' and 'communism', a central plank of the ideology of the National Party, is a direct challenge to the integrity of the church.

The gravity of the situation has been reflected in the World Reformed Alliance's declaration that apartheid is a heresy. The weight of this declaration should not be underestimated. Within Christian tradition, heresy implies a total rejection, an absolute division by which the church repudiates utterly a particular formulation of the gospel and the practice that grows out of it.

On 25 September 1985, a group of over 150 prominent Christians produced the *Kairos Document*. It demanded that the churches unequivocally take the side of the oppressed majority. It is in this spirit that *South Africa in the 1980s* is presented in this third edition:

'The time has come. The moment of truth has arrived. South Africa has been plunged into a crisis that is shaking the foundations and there is every indication that the crisis has only just begun and that it will deepen and become even more threatening in the months to come. It is the KAIROS or moment of truth not only for apartheid but also for the church.'

February 1986

Part I
Apartheid and The National Security State

The Roots of Apartheid

South African society is based on a system of apartheid sustained by a large state bureaucracy. Alone of all governments on the African continent, the white South African regime is engaged on a massive programme of social engineering reaching into the lives of all its black citizens.

Wealth, income and ownership are concentrated heavily in the hands of the white minority. The process began with white seizure of 85% of the land, and was reinforced as first mines and then industry were developed under white control. Africans, who are more than 70% of the population, received in 1980 just 29% of all personal income.

The apartheid groundplan's essential feature is the control of black labour through restrictive legislation and the concentration of huge numbers of the black population in areas designated as homelands, or 'independent states'. This control is made possible by the monopoly of political and military power in white hands. No less than three and a half million people were moved between 1960 and 1982 in order to implement this model.

The scale of this undertaking became apparent two decades ago with the 1960s boom in the South African economy. This resulted in a greater demand for black labour in the urban industrialised areas and stimulated increased migration from neighbouring states in southern Africa. In South Africa blacks were either forced by anti-squatter legislation from increasingly mechanised white farms, or were attracted from overpopulated rural areas by employment prospects in the towns. The drift from poverty-stricken countryside to overcrowded township accelerated, giving rise to the familiar features of inhuman hostels and urban crime. Thus the internal dynamism of South Africa's industrialising economy acted, in important respects, in contradiction to the ideology and demands of apartheid, which would require separate development. More rigorous control over black labour became necessary while the principles of apartheid were proclaimed as moral values and reinforced. On top of permanent black urban dwellers around the major towns came a flood of migrants. Their flow was regulated by draconian influx control mechanisms which ensured that only the 'economically useful' (predominantly men) were given access to the towns while 'appendages' (dependent wives and children in particular) were obliged by law to remain in the rural areas.

Meanwhile black unemployment was reaching alarming proportions. South Africa has been unable to maintain a steady growth rate since the early 1970s for a variety of reasons: the quadrupling of oil prices, world recession, fluctuations in the price of gold, the disincentive to foreign investment resulting from urban unrest. Unemployment rose from around 12% in 1971 to perhaps 21% in 1981. Periods of economic boom have merely slowed the trend, with new investment largely in labour-saving machinery. Between 1981 and 1984 a further 220,000 joined the ranks of some three million unemployed. The current economic crisis accelerates the process. In October 1984, for example, the chief executive of the National Maize Producers' Association advised white farmers to meet their economic difficulties by sacking workers and evicting the unwanted: 'Farmers can no longer afford to allow their farms to be used as slums,' he declared.

Government's principal response to this threat was to accelerate its 'independence' programme for the homelands whereby responsibility for maintaining an unemployed labour pool in rural areas fell on 'independent' black politicians, in practice a new tier of poorly disguised functionaries of the white minority superstate. Transkei, Bophuthatswana and Venda were created in rapid succession in the last years of the decade. Ciskei followed in 1981 and Kwandebele is promised for 1986.

With world recession, high inflation and the introduction of labour-saving technology, the need to turn back the tide of work-seekers coming into South Africa's towns and new industrial centres in the 'border' areas has not lessened. The dominance of a large state apparatus to staff a growing body of repressive and controlling legislation and the push to expand the present growth-oriented, maldistributive development strategy into all southern Africa have not been deflected by international protest. Computer control of labour was introduced in the Ciskei and is adding a new refinement as workers are carefully monitored for work record and docility. New 'development' areas have been proposed by Mr P.W. Botha, planned to cut across the 'borders' of 'independent states', and clearly illustrating the economic structure underlying the façade of bantustan sovereignty.

With growing white affluence, black rural poverty increases. Even in relatively 'well-off' Bophuthatswana, three-fifths of the population earn less than the bare minimum Household Subsistence Level; in one of the more prosperous townships of the Transkei, the figure is 76%. The bantustans are rural slums rather than farming areas. Over half their population is unemployed, and over three-quarters of bantustan income is from migrant labour in 'white' South Africa. Inflation, which is expected to exceed 20% in 1986, erodes purchasing power. The consequences are malnutrition, disease and death. 55% of all African deaths in South Africa are of children under the age of five, compared to just 7% for whites.*

---

*See *The South African Disease* by Cedric de Beer, SARS/CIIR, 1986.

16

The growing impoverishment of this majority contrasts with the relative affluence of a small but significant black minority, recipients of large wage increases that have begun to reduce the white-black wage gap. But in urban areas, as in rural, unemployment and inflation are biting. They have fuelled popular resistance, which has expressed itself in a number of different forms: riots, uprisings, boycotts, refusal to pay rent and bus fare increases, strikes, support for guerrilla movements and the growth of new political organisations. The need to contain such resistance and to suppress the universal desire for civil and political rights has led to a movement in the direction of a national security state, a phenomenon found in several Third World countries with similar deformities in their economic life. It was accompanied by major government efforts to restructure the apparatus of power enforcing apartheid.

National Security Ideology

While these movements were at first only one element in the dominant ideology of separate development, they grew into a major theme of Afrikaner thinking. 'National Security' and the 'total strategy' against what is called 'communism' now openly override some of the more superficial aspects of apartheid.*

Nonetheless, the basic goals of apartheid, white supremacy and the subordination of black economic, social and political needs to minority interests remain unchanged. The means of achieving them are hotly debated to the point of creating a major rift in the ruling Afrikaner elite. A call for entrenchment comes from the right wing, the so-called *verkramptes*, and the new Conservative Party. The call for 'modernisation' comes from leaders of the business world and from the South African Defence Force, each of which have powerful spokesmen in the National Party.

In the last decade the South African Defence Force has become a powerful voice in government, having grown into an efficient instrument for conventional warfare, *blitzkrieg* as in the 1976 and 1981 Angolan invasions, and counter-insurgency. This evolution of a

---

*The term 'communism' denotes in South African government thought a wide spectrum of political dissent from liberal reform to Marxist revolution. African nationalism is generally equated simply with communism. Thus, the ANC (African National Congress) is widely viewed by whites as an agent of 'Soviet imperialism'. ANC's non-military projects receive financial backing from Swedish, Danish, Dutch and Austrian government aid agencies. It has the support of the Socialist International, and strong links with both the Soviet Union and Social Democrat Parties in Europe.

small army into a powerful force with some 480,000 men at varying degrees of military preparedness in response to threats facing the state was accompanied by the rapid rise of Magnus Malan through the ranks in the 1970s. He became the chief ideologue of the South African National Security state and Minister of Defence in August 1980. Through his efforts a major revamping of the country's armed forces took place. His strength and that of the military establishment were augmented by two other important developments: the discrediting of the rival BOSS intelligence agency and its leader General Van den Bergh in the wake of the 'Information' scandal, and the development of South Africa's nuclear capacity.

The 'Information' scandal was the revelation that BOSS (the Bureau of State Security) had been covertly funding the dissemination of propaganda through the Department of Information. Large sums of money had been given to agents, and no account could be given of its use. Perhaps its most important result was to bring to power the most persuasive advocate of 'national security', Mr P.W. Botha, who had been Minister of Defence.

Under Mr Botha the State Security Council (SSC) has become a senior cabinet committee, increasingly dominating government decision-making. The SSC, with a large independent secretariat, gives effective expression to the idea of 'total strategy', with the participation of key military leaders, who are said to dominate its deliberations. The Chief of Staff, Intelligence, in the SADF, Lt.Gen. Van der Westhuizen, holds the key post of Secretary to the SSC, while his predecessor in the job, another general, has been sent as 'ambassador' to the Ciskei. The military are also represented on 15 inter-departmental policy-planning committees serving the cabinet. The SSC would be capable of taking control of government if Parliament were suspended, and both Mr Botha and military spokesmen have alluded to tensions between democratic structures and the needs of national security. Several commentators foresee more overt military rule if the splits in the Afrikaner elite become too debilitating for Afrikanerdom.

There is mounting evidence that the West German aided research at Pelindaba, the Valindaba uranium enrichment plant, and military contacts with Israel have now given South Africa the ability to deliver nuclear warheads. It has been suggested that three sites, Walvis Bay, Voortrekkerhoogte and the St Lucia region of Natal are earmarked for missiles directed respectively at the West African coastal cities, Central Africa and East Africa/Madagascar. The nuclear reactor at Koeberg designed to produce plutonium will vastly increase South Africa's capacity to develop a nuclear arsenal. A flash observed at sea and the development of long-range howitzers indicate that South Africa will shortly be in possession of effective tactical nuclear weapons. Coupled with sophisticated tracking technology at the

Simonstown naval communications centre and the building of new underground airforce installations in the eastern Transvaal, these developments give growing weight to the voice of the Defence Force in the counsels of the state.

The militarisation of the South African state is reflected in massive leaps in defence expenditure, from a budget of two billion Rand at the beginning of the 1980s to over four billion in 1986. South Africa now has the largest and best equipped army on the African continent, exceeding that of Nigeria, which fought a civil war and has three times its population, and more than all the neighbouring Frontline states' military resources put together. The real defence costs, which should include a further 1½ billion Rand spent annually on weapons manufacture, and half a billion spent on police, are difficult to estimate because of numerous hidden purchases of arms and equipment from Western countries through intermediaries. The South African police, set for rapid expansion to 68,000 by the end of the 1980s, plays a paramilitary role in townships.

The creation of the parastatal ARMSCOR and the rapid building of industrial plant and armaments factories by private enterprise have made South Africa self-sufficient in much conventional weaponry. The government concept of 'strategic economic programming for national defence' is bringing the country's economic life increasingly under the domination of military imperatives. This is creating on a smaller scale the military-industrial complex of the USA and Soviet Union, and was reflected in the creation of a Defence Advisory Council containing key industrialists and the secondment of the deputy chief executive of Barlow Rand to head ARMSCOR.

The philosophy of 'national security' and 'total strategy' attempts therefore to bring together both military and industrial interests. In this scheme of things other priorities, in particular human, civil and political rights, are subordinate to the national interest. A state bureaucracy and a small political clique effectively undermine the independence of the judiciary. Military and police authorities attempt to manipulate, control or coerce the mass media into preparing the public for military incursions into neighbouring states and highlighting supposed threats to national security. Press freedom is curtailed until almost no aspects of state repression can be reported and even the names of detainees may be withheld. Distinctions between paramilitary police and army blur. Not only do they look the same but areas of civil disorder become 'operational areas', the military term for regions of guerrilla incursion, out of bounds to all but selected journalists. Press, radio and television require police escorts to report on township disorder, and face ten years in jail for illegal reporting of boycotts, strikes and rioting.

From October 1984, when 7,000 troops were sent in to occupy Sebokeng township, joint police-military occupation and patrolling of townships became permanent. The militarisation of white youth in classroom Youth Preparedness courses and in cadet training, and the widespread purchase of arms by whites since the beginning of serious urban disorders in mid-1984, means that whites, in and out of uniform, behave as if they are participants in a civil war. The declaration of a state of emergency on 21 July 1985 and the subsequent increase in state violence against black citizens led the Anglican, Roman Catholic, Methodist and United Congregational Churches to consider withdrawing uniformed chaplains from the SADF. For the first time, the state was showing no particular favour to the Churches, arresting even leaders like Rev. Allan Boesak as well as other lesser known local Christian leaders and community workers.

Christianity under this ideology is required to serve the state because the state has its own idiosyncratic version of its refusal to acknowledge African political rights. 'It is a struggle of the Christian western civilisation against the powers of darkness and Marxism and not just a black/white struggle,' Mr P.W. Botha has said. The same claims were made in Zimbabwe and their falsity has been amply demonstrated.

The impact of militarisation on society is being felt by both black and white communities. Citizen Force duties, after an initial two-year period of conscription, have been extended to 720 days spread over twelve years. This involves some quarter of a million men; in all, almost half the white male population between the ages of 17 and 55 is engaged in some kind of national security activity for periods of the year. A further 300,000 young people are involved in military cadet training programmes. All Churches but the large and powerful Nederduitse Gereformeerde Kerk (NGK) and its white splinter Churches have taken a stand against the 1983 Defence Amendment Act that divides conscientious objectors into 'religious' and 'political' categories. 'Political objectors' are now subject to six years' imprisonment for refusal to serve in the armed forces, while the former are subject to lengthy and repressive forms of alternative service.

The Act was the government response to Christian war resisters who had gone to jail and detention barracks, and had led to church demands for alternative forms of service and recognition of the right to conscientious objection. The Namibian-Angolan war that is costing countless African lives is making a major impact on whites through the growing number of casualties amongst conscripts, and the growth of Christian protest in South Africa. The church-supported End Conscription Campaign (EEC), now calling for troops to leave black townships, has strongly reinforced this pressure through a successful public campaign. A very high percentage of young men are now failing to appear in the annual January call-up,

20

and the state has begun to link the EEC with the ANC as a major threat to national security.

The South African Defence Force has also taken over areas of the northern Transvaal and northern Natal. This has resulted in a large-scale movement of people, either to deny guerrillas a welcoming population, or to make secure massive new military installations planned for the region. The experience of the Makgato people, forced from their home in 1979, has added a new dimension to 'social engineering', that of population removals for military ends. Such an uprooting of communities is likely to become more common. In response the ANC began laying landmines in border regions in late 1985, causing white casualties. Already the pattern of shut-down farms and security checks, reminiscent of the war in Zimbabwe, is appearing along most borders. To combat the impact of military repression in border areas, 'hearts and minds' programmes are carried out, if it is decided to let the population stay. This attempt to soften the military image is paralleled nationally by the use of troops in a wide range of civilian occupations.

The ideology of national security has drawn South Africa into association with other states that share, to some degree, this philosophy: Chile, Taiwan, South Korea, Paraguay, and Israel. The basis for this alignment is economic or military co-operation and trade. In the case of warm relationships with Taiwan and Argentina under the generals the bait has been South African uranium. A South African-South American Chamber of Commerce was set up in 1979 while General Magnus Malan visited Latin American military leaders. South African exports to the area rose from 6.8 million Rand in value in 1966 to 172.2 million in 1977; a comparable leap in South African-Israeli trade took place in the 1970s. There are now South African embassies in thirteen Latin American countries while Chile maintains strong naval links also. The growth of this *de facto* 'fourth bloc' alignment has provided South Africa with a group of like-minded trading partners in the event of any breakdown in trade with Britain, the EEC and the USA in response to United Nations economic sanctions, should they be imposed.

Relationships within the 'fourth bloc' reinforce South Africa's movement towards the position of a national security state. But the process in the southern African context has in-built constraints. A total strategy involves a 'united and collective effort which includes diplomacy, politics, economics, industry, local authorities and the military', according to General Malan. It requires some degree of co-operation and consent from blacks. Black people, troops, informers and political collaborators, co-opted, lured or coerced into supporting white rule, prolonged the life of the minority regime in Rhodesia. The creation of a black middle class with a stake in the system, and the accelerated formation of black regiments, became priorities for South Africa's military strategists. Today over a quarter of the South African regular forces are blacks with the 'tribal' regiments of the 'independent states' earmarked for an important proxy role in counter-insurgency. The 'Minister of Defence' of Bophuthatswana is, for example, a white South African, Brigadier Hennie Riekert, who in 1980 presided over a defence budget of 3.8 million Rand, 80% up on the previous year. Many of the high command of Transkei's army are ex-Selous Scouts from Rhodesia, while Israel provides the 'Ciskei airforce'.

To maintain the economic, social and political ascendancy of whites with the resultant unequal sharing of wealth between the white and other communities, the apartheid system had to be remodelled. The resistance generated by the old model, particularly the 1973 Durban strikes and the 1976 urban uprisings, pointed to the urgency of the task. This remodelling was a military necessity for survival. Part of the constitutional strategy was to co-opt 'coloureds' and 'Indians' on to the white side of the apartheid divide. It failed: no leader of any stature joined Mr Botha's President's Council to plan reforms.

The form it finally took in the 1983 Constitution Bill was a three-chamber parliament with 45 seats for an 'Indian' chamber, 85 for 'coloureds' and 178 for whites. The three chambers elected members to an electoral college on the same 4:2:1 ratio so that it comprised 50 whites, 25 'coloureds' and 13 'Indians'. In September 1984 this college elected Mr P.W. Botha as executive president with near-dictatorial powers. He is serving a seven-year term and successful impeachment is extremely difficult. A President's Council of 60 members, 25 nominated by the President, the rest elected on the 4:2:1 ratio, discuss affairs defined by the President as 'common to all racial groups'.

The purpose of the new constitution is twofold. Most important, it finally confirms the exclusion of 'Africans' from political rights in South Africa other than at town-council level. 'Indians' and 'coloureds' are summoned to close ranks with whites in the extended *laager*. Secondly, an executive presidency, dominated by the military, fits the 'modernising autocracy' favoured by President Reagan's advisers as a solution to the problem of revolution in the Third World. On the one hand the powers of the South African state have been increased yet further to repress black revolt; on the other, the capacity of *verkrampte* reaction to block 'reform' would, it was hoped, decrease in the face of strong presidential rule.

The need for these new priorities was equally perceived by industry and commerce from the changing exigencies of profitability. After military demands the second important set of pressures on the state has come from the transnational corporations. These pressures are of the utmost significance for the apartheid system since they are

22

exerted at its Achilles' heel, the skilled black worker and urban resident.

Industrial and Commercial Interests

South Africa is still greatly dependent for its economic growth on foreign investment and particularly the advanced technology brought by the transnationals. In 1984 alone private business enterprises spent 14bn Rand in new fixed investment, new plant and machinery. The public sector invested almost as much, some of it financed by loans. Though there has been a net flow out of South Africa in six of the last nine years, foreign capital remains very important. At the start of 1985 foreign investors owned 67 billion Rands' worth of assets in South Africa, one third of it investment in South Africa's public sector. The 'private' and 'public' sectors are, of course, intricately linked. South Africa's largest chemical company SENTRACHEM, for example, represents a partnership between British Petroleum and the state-owned Industrial Development Corporation.

Nonetheless, in the past, there has been a degree of conflict between the interests of the large transnationals and those of the National Party that governed South Africa. An important element in this conflict has been the divergence between the interests of the white working class, which has traditionally been represented in the National Party, and the demands of big business. Shortfalls of skilled workers throughout the South African economy now stand at over 6%. These have been created by the complexity of modern extractive and manufacturing industry against a background of inadequate education and restricted employment opportunities for blacks. They have been aggravated by the proportion of working time spent by skilled white workers in different forms of military duty, which in some industries is estimated at 7-12%. In response, the transnationals have sought a less repressive climate for industrial relations, a controlled unionisation of labour in the wake of the 1973 Durban strikes, and the creation of a skilled, stable black work force. The changes required to bring this about have consistently been seen as a threat by white workers and continue to be fiercely resisted by their political spokesmen in the National, Conservative and Herstigte Nasionale parties.

However, the size and voice of the white working class has progressively diminished in the last decade. Many white workers have moved up into quasi-managerial and supervisory positions.

23

Afrikaner businessmen, traditionally the poor cousins of English-speaking South African entrepreneurs, have come to dominate the caucuses of the National Party and redirect its priorities. Always an important element in the National Party and Broederbond, their growing purchase on the commanding heights of the South African economy has augmented their power. Afrikaner business houses are now challenging the monopoly of English-speakers, assuming their ideology and goals, and redefining identities. Of the seven business groups which now dominate the economy, two, Sanlam and Rembrandt, are in origin Afrikaner. Among banks, for example, Nedbank with 8.1bn Rand assets in 1982, Bankorp with 6.7 billion and Volkskas with 6.1 billion were hard on the heels of Barclays (10.8 billion) and Stanbic (8.4 billion), even if still lagging behind the combined financial muscle of the companies in the Anglo/De Beers group. The Rembrandt conglomerate, headed by an Afrikaner, Anton Rupert, is now the 15th biggest firm in the country. Founded on tobacco and beer, it is a classic example of an Afrikaner-led transnational whose interests are today finding a home in the National Party. Above all, South African business has become increasingly concentrated and interlinked, with just seven corporations controlling 80% of the capitalisation of the Johannesburg Stock Exchange. Thus, though much of South African business is technically in 'foreign' hands, the relationships between capitalist enterprises are complex. South Africa is a major secondary capitalist centre in which divisions between 'Afrikaner' and 'English' business and finance are of decreasing significance.

While differences between international business interests and Afrikanerdom were instrumental, in part, in bringing the National Party to power in 1948, today this conflict has split both the National Party and Afrikanerdom itself. Ever since the 1930s, the distinction between the 'economic rationality' of enlightened English business on one hand and the rural philosophy of bigoted Afrikaner apartheid on the other has been largely mythical. Afrikanerdom finds its reflection today as much in the Sanlam sky-scrapers of its major cities as in the ox-cart.

The business community at first believed that Mr P.W. Botha could navigate a transition from an older racial capitalism to more liberal forms of capitalism on a Brazilian model. A 1979 Conference at the Carlton Centre between leaders of government and business seemed to chart a way forward, and formed a high-water mark of business confidence in his capacity to steer the necessary changes in the face of *verkrampte* strategies. His speech to the Natal Congress of the National Party in August 1985, which promised no changes of significance, was a corresponding low-water mark, confirming their growing fear of his impotence and lack of direction. The business community now urgently seek a new perhaps federally structured

South Africa, and the elimination of what they see as the costly and damaging irrationality of the apartheid bureaucracy.

The business community's worries are reinforced by the current economic prospects for South Africa, especially after the September 1985 foreign loans crisis which nearly brought down a prominent bank. State expenditure is a constant target of business criticism, but the state has repeatedly proved unable to cut back, because the military, the bantustans and 'reform' itself are all very costly. The result, when combined with the collapse in the value of the Rand, will be sharply increased inflation. When renewed inflation is added to rapidly rising unemployment, the political consequences in the townships are clear. Meanwhile the international pariah status of South Africa prevents new foreign borrowing, and risks further turmoil. Exporters, though much helped by the lower Rand, face the possibility of political boycotts, even in what in 1984 had seemed a bright prospect, the neighbouring countries of southern Africa. The strategy of the business community is therefore now being put forward with added urgency and considerable international support from the west.

Neither P.W. Botha's nor the business strategy, though, is aimed at bringing about a fundamental transformation of apartheid or the removal of its intrinsic injustices. Business leaders frequently reiterate their opposition to one person-one vote. The social concerns of the transnationals are byproducts of quite different goals, cost effectiveness and profitability. The priorities of the Defence Force are determined by the prospect of an expanding guerrilla war. However, the control and productivity of black labour, and the 'stability' demanded by investor and military alike, both require that concessions be made to the black professional and labour elite.

Within this limited prospectus, social and political changes were planned by Mr P.W. Botha's government. The rise of strong unregistered black unions in the 1970s provided a spur to bring unions into the 'protective and stabilising elements of the system', to quote Wiehahn. Some of the Wiehahn Commission's 1979 recommendations have now been put into practice, thereby giving the green light to the development of black unions. The original aim was to channel and control militant unionism by legal restrictions such as the need for unions to be registered. This, however, was strongly opposed by some of the key emergent unions and had to be abandoned, as the early 1980s saw an unprecedented level of labour unrest, greater than the Durban strikes of 1973.

Likewise, the Riekert Commission, presented to the world in the aura of new reforms, had as its main goal to tighten up influx control while ironing out sources of irritation for a minority of privileged black urban workers and professional men. Against the promise of better and permanent housing, with some security of tenure for the black urban few, stand measures that heavily penalise employers of 'illegal' workers and drive migrants back into the homelands. By 1980, according to estimates, over 50,000 'illegal' workers had already been expelled from South Africa's towns as a result of the Commission's provisions. The number of arrests for influx control offences doubled between 1980 and 1982.

The combined impact of the Wiehahn and Riekert Commissions has been to relegate 'surplus population' more efficiently to the homelands while catering for the formation of the stable, trained urban workforce demanded by the state and private enterprise. The future needs of modern industry are likely to sustain this momentum towards the creation of a small, relatively privileged group of urban blacks, in default of an adequate supply of white skilled workers. Average black earnings outside agriculture rose an average 13% a year between 1975 and 1982 (2% in real terms). In manufacturing, African average earnings rose from R57 per month in 1971 to R255 in 1981. That was still less than a quarter of average white earnings in manufacturing, but considerably more than Africans could earn in the 'homelands' or on white-owned farms. Most of the transnational companies have training schemes to provide token black representation in management. In keeping with Riekert's suggestions, black adult education got 180% more funds, secondary school and technical education 55% more, and black housing in 'white' areas 29% more during 1980. Middle-class blacks are getting 99-year leases on their homes, and the possibility of freehold in the future. Soweto's reward for the police violence of 1976 has been a major electrification scheme and the promise of six exclusive, fee-paying schools to be built by the major corporations.

This strategy won considerable support from the international as well as local business community. The Fordville model of development, a luxurious housing estate for black professional families outside Port Elizabeth, fitted both the prestige project requirements of the transnationals and the objectives of government. Business had already embarked on a range of 'pilot' schemes for urban blacks, such as the promotion of site-and-service areas, and established an Urban Foundation to push these forward. As the crisis deepened in 1985, one of the responses was a November meeting of international and South African business leaders to intensify these efforts to be visibly 'helping blacks'.

The government agenda included the removal of some petty apartheid, though this was to be by application from individual institutions and dependent on racial attitudes in the white community. For example, only a small minority of hotels and restaurants have requested permission to become multi-racial, and the repeal of the mixed marriages acts only touches a tiny minority. Similarly the access of blacks to new jobs will depend on successful

26

negotiation with white unions over 'closed shop' agreements.

Thus the state bureaucracy will continue to keep control of black labour by instituting 'reforms' by application rather than through enabling legislation. The movement towards greater emphasis on private enterprise means that the essential functions of the apartheid system will be shared with others: white employers and the new political elite of the 'independent' homelands. For example some 2,000 people were detained in Transkei in 1985. In the Eastern Cape, businessmen negotiated troop withdrawals from townships to end consumer boycotts.

But, under the pressure of uncontrollable urban unrest and the threat of international sanctions, there is now serious talk of the restoration of a limited form of black citizenship to classes of South African citizens relegated to bantustans since 1976. Similarly, new methods of controlling the influx of work-seekers, for example through access to freehold housing, have been mooted. Such concessions are demanded by a private enterprise now shocked by the spectre of imminent revolution and widespread instability.

The 1980s began with the National Party not so much the party of Afrikanerdom but the party of militarism and private enterprise. The direction of current legislation points both to the reinforcement of divisions within the black community and to growing repression. The most obvious of the divisions created by apartheid policies is that between rural and urban blacks, between migrant labour and permanent township residents, between rich and poor. Per capita state expenditure on black education in rural and urban areas was equal in 1976. By 1980-1981, however, the African 'homelands' were only receiving 73 Rand per black child compared with 190 Rand per black child in white areas, which of course include the white farms, where education is very poor, as well as urban areas. Only the Ciskei had a higher per capita expenditure than the urban areas, and it was a major supplier of labour for South African industry. Regions like Lebowa were receiving as little as 36 Rand per child for education. Freehold housing in townships will be in the expensive upper range accessible only to the wealthy in the rural areas.

The tendency towards larger disparities in wealth within the black community is likely to continue. The development strategy adopted by the South African government has the clear political intention of co-opting a relatively affluent small black middle-class while relegating an impoverished majority to the policing of 'independent homelands' militia. The often repeated remark that in South Africa north and south meet is true, and National Party policies attempt to sustain this division in perpetuity in an area where it is susceptible of resolution.

Regional Objectives: Extending the Laager

The insertion of the 'independent homelands' into a wider constellation of states under the economic sway of South Africa was announced as the lynchpin of Mr Botha's foreign policy in 1979. This policy aimed at retaining the economic dependence of the states of Southern Africa on South Africa, thereby limiting their political options. It has been backed by a series of economic squeezes and military sabotage of the economies of the genuinely independent states, whose Southern African Development Co-ordination Conference (SADCC) stands in clear opposition to the constellation dream.*

The constellation of states was warmly welcomed by the international business community. The transnationals saw in the plan an uncontentious expression of their normal method of working, in which national differences and frontiers offer opportunities rather than limitations.

However, the unexpected sweeping victory of ZANU (PF) in the Rhodesian elections of February 1980 set limits on the realisation of Mr Botha's foreign policy. The long-term prospects for a Pretoria-based constellation of states suffered a rude setback as the independent states of southern Africa began co-ordinating their economies through SADCC, which formed a permanent secretariat in Gaborone in 1983. It was in this context that South Africa stepped up the alternative policy of destabilising its recalcitrant neighbours (a policy in which it had never relented in Angola). SADCC's key projects in its aim of reducing dependence are the railway lines to Mozambican and Angolan ports; they became the main targets for sabotage, so that by 1984 only one of the four lines was in regular operation. The region's traffic was forced back through South Africa.

By 1984 it seemed that destabilisation had forced the constellation of states back on to the agenda. A security accord between Mozambique and South Africa was signed at Nkomati amid great pomp. The leaders of South African business were present to mark their approval. Earlier, in Lusaka, Angola and South Africa had concluded an agreement providing for the withdrawal of South African troops from Angola. These initiatives allowed P.W. Botha to embark on a tour of European capitals, where he presented South Africa as a regional power. In his speech at Nkomati, he had once again spoken of a constellation.

---

*For details of this strategy, see Joseph Hanlon, *Apartheid Power in southern Africa*, CIIR/James Currey, 1986.

Yet a year later South Africa's intentions at Nkomati had become clearer. President Machel, who at Nkomati itself had reaffirmed Mozambique's commitment to SADCC, found that the SADF continued to support the MNR rebels in flagrant violation of the Nkomati Accord. South African troops held on in Angola, used airpower and troops in support of UNITA, and launched a raid on the capital of Botswana. At a meeting in September 1985 the Frontline states announced their willingness to see sanctions imposed on South Africa. Their position had, nonetheless, been tragically weakened by President Reagan's support for UNITA in the misguided belief that Angola's problems were a local reflection of East-West conflict. This strengthened Pretoria and infuriated the Frontline state leaders in Lusaka. Lusaka has remained the bellwether of the region: in 1980 it saw the founding conference of SADCC, in 1984 the disengagement agreement between Angola and South Africa, in 1985 a meeting between South African business leaders and the ANC, and in early 1986 a meeting at which the foreign ministers of the Frontline states complained bitterly to their EEC colleagues about the ineffectiveness of European policy.

The South African regional dream, though, was finally shattered by internal urban unrest. On the one hand, the military struck out at what it claimed to be external bases of terrorism, unable to accept that the roots of unrest lie in apartheid South Africa itself. On the other hand, strong Western pressure on SADCC states to sign accords with Pretoria evaporated as police violence destroyed P.W. Botha's status as supposed 'peacemaker'. Accordingly South Africa resorted again to direct destabilisation. A second commando raid was launched against Lesotho in December 1985, followed in January by an economic blockade. As the pressure built up, the Lesotho prime minister was deposed in a coup, and the new government negotiated with South Africa and airlifted ANC refugees out of the country.

State Violence

The first half of the 1980s has seen the South African government respond to internal democratic opposition with consistent repression. The decade began with the killing of over 60 young people on 17 June 1980, and progressed to a total of about 700 killed as a result of the unrest in the year to October 1985. In between there had been a steady stream of deaths in detention, including those of key trades unionists Dr Neil Aggett and Andries Raditsela. Battered by permanent labour militancy on the one hand and the swelling white backlash on the other, Mr Botha's policies now lie in ruins. Instructively, the bantustans have followed the overall trends in South Africa with vicious repression in Ciskei, the Transkei and Bophuthatswana. The brutality of the authorities in the Ciskei, particularly in the vast township of Mdantsane, has reached horrifying proportions. During 1983 the civilian population was subjected to a reign of terror by the Ciskei authorities and their vigilantes. Between July and September 90 people were reported killed as a result of the authorities' violent response to a bus boycott. In some townships hit squads have claimed victims amongst local leaders of the UDF and its affiliates. In 1985 white police shot indiscriminately into crowds in the townships of Langa, Crossroads, Queenstown and Mamelodi, in the last apparently from a helicopter.

The decision to impose a state of emergency was a further counsel of despair from a government whose policies had been destroyed by violent popular protest, organised resistance from the UDF, and opposition from the black trades unions. The state hoped to crush UDF organisation outside the glare of publicity created by treason trials, and under the guise of establishing 'law and order' in rioting townships. They acted swiftly; security police raided the houses of UDF leaders within 24 hours of a press briefing by Mr P.W. Botha on the morning of 21 July 1985. During the first two weeks 86% of those arrested were prominent in the UDF or in its affiliates. On average during the first month, about 120 people were arrested and four killed daily, and the rate remained high in subsequent months.

The state of emergency exacerbated tensions between the business community and National Party. The splits within the white power bloc became increasingly evident; the spectre of economic sanctions, consumer boycotts against white shops, police violence and the growing alienation of white workers affected big business and the National Party differently. For several months the state appeared directionless, rudderless, merely responding to black resistance and unable to take any initiative. This was nowhere more dramatically illustrated than in the State President's infamous 'Rubicon speech' of 15 August. Great international expectations had been created by a preview of the speech by the Foreign Minister, Pik Botha, in Europe. In the event, despite the presence of the world's mass media, the speech was directed at a conservative Natal Party Congress with limited taste for concrete 'reforms'. The moment of truth revealed the State President in his true colours, the small-town political fixer, playing to the *verkrampte* gallery.

The realisation that P.W. Botha was condemned to strut on the stage of history while South Africa's townships burnt had, however, dawned earlier on the business world. They had put out feelers in

A young woman shot by the South African Police after the funeral of 3-year old Mitah Ngobeni, also killed by the police.

Inkatha members patrolling alongside the police at a UDF rally (Lamontville).

Catholic seminarians march on the Union building to deliver a letter of protest to the State President.

A car is overturned and burnt in the barricades in a disturbance at Athlone, a 'coloured' suburb of Cape Town.

National Union of Mineworkers supporters at the conference at Welkom.

Students at the University of the Witwatersrand demonstrating against the imposition of the State of Emergency.

Students defy the army and police during the boycott at the University of the Western Cape.

The SADF moves into Athlone.

NUM leaders James Motlhasi and Jeffrey Madida at a rally at Jabulari Ampitheatre.

The launch of COSATU, the new trade union federation.

Angry youths on the march after clashes with police at Bongani Khumalo's funeral, Soweto.

Helen Joseph at the End Conscription Campaign Fair.

Margaret NuPapha, head of the South African Domestic Workers' Association.

A FOSATU union meeting duing the strike at the Firestone plant.

April to President Kaunda to see if a meeting with the ANC could be arranged. They were followed in July by the Progressive Federal Party. P.W. Botha's blundering performance at the Natal Congress, following the death of 113 people in local rioting verging on insurrection, sent shock waves through the business world, finally shattering confidence. The Rand plummetted as two American banks refused to reschedule short term loans to the South African government. The governor of the Reserve Bank of South Africa, Gerhard de Kock, vainly toured Europe and the USA, getting a stony reception from bankers. A six-month moratorium was placed on the repayment of $7.5 billion of short term foreign debt falling due, and in a move hitherto avoided by even the most desperate debtor countries because of its damage to the country's credit rating, $6.5 billion of interbank deposits were frozen. In 1986 the moratorium was extended. South Africa's $22 billion foreign debt suddenly appeared as a major problem resolvable only through a return to stability.

But stability was precisely what the apartheid system could not guarantee. The State Security Council and the generals were convinced that this was the fault of the African National Congress whom they believed to be orchestrating disorder from Lusaka. In a sense, this was true. The voice of the ANC on Radio Freedom from Addis Ababa and Lusaka, listened to avidly by blacks in the townships, counselled mass resistance and insurrectionary tactics. But it was also clear that many of the township disturbances were spontaneous eruptions of popular anger, un-coordinated, often costly of young life, and certainly not directed by 'communists', who, where they existed, might have been expected to place a premium on curbing anarchic violence and creating disciplined organisation.

Military Intelligence was caught trying to blow up Gulf Oil installations, and diaries captured from the MNR rebels showed it to be embroiled in Mozambique supporting a terrorist movement with arms and advice. The generals were increasingly pursuing their own foreign policy. Whether it coincided with that of P.W. Botha was not always easy to detect. The appointment of General Jannie Geldenhuys in place of the retiring General Constand Viljoen gave some indication of the future direction of the SSC. Geldenhuys, in the skewed spectrum of South African politics, was a 'liberal' general. Unlike Viljoen, he did not nurture fantasies of quick victory against liberation movements with widespread popular support. Given his experience in 'total strategy' tactics towards the Frontline states, his appointment to head the SADF was an indication that more subtle approaches to the ANC might be tolerated by the military.

In mid-September the chairman of Anglo-American, Gavin Relly, led a delegation of businessmen to Lusaka for discussions with the leaders of the ANC. A month later PFP leader, Van Zyl Slabbert, followed. The Relly meeting had been approved by the State President after he had been approached by Dr F. du Plessis, chairman of the powerful Afrikaner Sanlam conglomerate. So, notwithstanding P.W. Botha's later repudiation of the meeting, it was not, in itself, a sign of the rift between the business world and the National Party. It was probably approved in the hope that probing about 'socialism' and the ANC's relationship with the South African Communist Party might create tension in the leadership. If the intention was to damage the ANC, it failed miserably. The two meetings smoothed the path for successful ANC talks in London with international business leaders and an appearance before the Commons Select Committee on Foreign Affairs. They also served to demythologise the ANC and provide its leader, Oliver Tambo, with a degree of legitimacy within white South Africa.

The talks were exploratory but showed a certain progression. Van Zyl Slabbert left his meeting on 19 October endorsing a precise ANC demand: release of political prisoners, not only Nelson Mandela. The hidden agenda on the side of big business was the launching on 21 September of a Convention Alliance and the optimistic hope that the ANC might be talked into not attacking it. An odd hybrid of some 150 South Africans seeking negotiation on South Africa's future through a national convention, the Convention Alliance was essentially Inkatha and the PFP. Neither was politically acceptable to the ANC. Inkatha had been turned into a battering ram to bludgeon democratic opposition in Natal. The PFP agreed in principle to put up candidates in the ethnic tri-cameral parliament in the 'Indian' and 'coloured' chambers. The 'moderate centre' lasted only a few weeks before Inkatha and the PFP withdrew, acknowledging the failure of the 'Anglo-Zulu alliance' by which the business community set such great store. The convention idea, however, remains.

With a growing number of countries setting off on the path of minor economic sanctions, and no sign that the insurrection in South Africa's townships was being quelled, Mr P.W. Botha's options remain limited. There must be a temptation to cut and run from Namibia, where the cost of the war in a time of national crisis is increasingly high. The planned increased recruitment of 11,000 police in 1986 indicates the strain under which the state is operating to contain urban unrest. The tens of thousands of troops in Ovamboland would be a welcome addition to the army of occupation in the townships. Withdrawal from Namibia could be packaged as a major statesmanlike gesture to reduce pressure for stronger sanctions. But the generals do not want to leave UNITA to defeat, or to the CIA, who now have permission and money to fund it. The surge of black hope which would be created by a SWAPO government in Windhoek doubtless would worry the military.

Mr Botha would also be deterred by the impact of 'giving up

Namibia' on his already eroding white electoral support. The victory of the right-wing Herstigte Nasionale Party in Sasolburg in an October 1985 by-election was some measure of the disenchantment of the white working class with his policies. They saw their jobs at risk from blacks. For the first time for decades there are significant numbers of unemployed whites, with the figure doubling between 1984 and 1985.* Right wing dissent is rife in the police force, especially in the lower ranks. The result is more police violence, which itself fuels the insurrection. The 1985 uprising in Athlone, Cape Town, for example, was triggered by more aggressive police activity following the appointment of a new Conservative Party chief of police.

The inexorable erosion of Mr P.W. Botha's support and his inability to satisfy the business community mean that his early retirement becomes a distinct possibility. In the week after his 'Rubicon speech' 1,700 South Africans applied to the Australian embassy to emigrate. The counter-insurgency experts like chief of police Coetzee and the head of the SADF, Geldenhuys, need a plausible national leader acceptable to Afrikaner intellectuals and business leaders. The most likely candidate is Gerrit Viljoen, considered the intellectual equal of anyone in the SSC, ex-head of the Broederbond, with experience in forcing through change in the face of right-wing opposition. However, the conservative Transvaal National Party leader, F.W. de Klerk, has built himself considerable support in the succession race. The alternative is reinforcement of naked repression in a Pinochet-style coup, though this would clearly upset many in the business community.

Meanwhile the state appears ready to attempt to exhaust the young people of the townships, netting their leadership, punishing them by torture in prison, or killing them on the streets. The white left are also harassed by 'hidden' forms of repression: slashed tyres, attacks on houses, threats. As the draconian new censorship laws for the media and the growing number of deported or arrested journalists and roughed-up camera crews indicate, this will increasingly take place out of the public gaze. In a situation where the security forces use a penumbra of criminals to reach the targets in townships they cannot attack, the implications are frightening. Since the death in 1981 of Griffiths Mxenge, a human rights lawyer, 'disappearances' and unexplained political murders have marked the Eastern Cape. The murder of the Cradock leader Matthew Goniwe in June 1985 has come to symbolise this new phenomenon. Repression, as in Latin American countries, is likely therefore to turn next on church and

---

*Total *registered* white, 'coloured' and 'Asian' unemployed was 29,345 in July 1984 and 67,903 in July 1985. Significant numbers would not register, so the real figure is much higher.

human rights organisations which are able to report on police and security force brutality. At the same time security police will attempt to sponsor violent conflict between Inkatha on the one hand and the UDF and trades unions on the other, using Zulu chauvinism as a proxy for repression in Natal. In view of their shared interest in Inkatha, any lasting rift between the state and business community should not be exaggerated.

Restructuring apartheid under the prevailing system of limited white electoral politics has proved singularly difficult. The initiative now lies not with a National Party weakened by the trauma of transition caused by the changing economic conditions of the 1970s, but with the workers, students, trade unions and nationalist movements whose timescale for majority rule has suddenly shortened. The black nationalism that grew out of the 1970s is now more clearly than ever the main motor for change that will drive the troubled history of South Africa in the next decade.

Part II
The Future
of
Black Nationalism

The Black Consciousness Movement (BCM) 1969-1980

The changes South Africa experienced during the 1970s had a complex variety of causes. The consequences of major economic developments on white politics have already been emphasised, and their repercussions in the social engineering of apartheid discussed. But equally important has been the action of blacks themselves in bringing about change.

The unwillingness of rural Africans to accept impoverishment and their determination to seek work in towns has been at the root of apartheid's dilemma. The flood of blacks to urban areas during the 1970s swamped an inefficient bureaucracy of officials and courts; blacks sleeping rough in white areas looking for work increased to a point where Bantu Administration officers were obliged to turn a blind eye. The remodelling of influx control now proposed may be seen as a response to a virtual collapse of previous mechanisms. Low wages and unhealthy, inhuman working conditions lay at the heart of the Durban strikes and the growing unionisation of black labour, and these in turn forced the state to permit a union movement, now over half a million strong, and militant. The pressures from the radical black students in the 1976 disturbances led to a 180% increase in adult education funds in the 1980 budget. At every point it is black initiative which has been responsible for government attempts at concession or control.

Originally the Black Consciousness Movement (BCM) grew up through an increased realisation amongst black intellectuals of their own systematic exploitation and in reaction to white liberal paternalism, but it was fuelled by resistance to the government-sponsored ideology of ethnicity that was used to justify the bantustan programme. The Bantu Education System, designed to create a culturally subservient black population, was anathema. Yet the demands of an expanding economy were forcing ever growing numbers of young people through it. It was under the pressure of township life in the mid-1970s and the newly enforced Afrikaans language policy in black schools that the urban areas exploded in June 1976.

The 1976 urban revolts, of which Soweto is the best known, drove black nationalism in South Africa into a new era, characterised by increasing sophistication in the analysis of exploitation, particularly its economic roots, and in strategies for achieving political advancement.

The risings demonstrated two cardinal points to the black community:

37

1. the importance of politicised young people, their maturity and leadership qualities;
2. the limitations of the political consciousness and organisational abilities of school-age youth.

These limitations were of two kinds. The first was the absence of any long-term strategy or well-worked out analysis of the black predicament; the risings were spontaneous and, even when they were controlled by black consciousness activists, it was not always easy to understand the selection of targets. The philosophy of black consciousness, with its emphasis on psychological, cultural and economic liberation, gave few precise guidelines for action. Techniques such as the mass demonstration and stay-away were repeated to a point beyond their effectiveness as repression took its toll. The range of possible political action was strictly limited if BCM wished to survive 'above ground'.

The second problem was the gulf that had to be bridged between school pupils, students and workers. The use made of Zulu hostel dwellers, who were incited by the police to beat up Soweto residents and quell student unrest, was a brutal demonstration of one weakness of the movement. It was the police, rather than the students, who operated effectively in terms of the divisions created by apartheid within the black community. The young students failed to obtain united support from workers. The unity of the black experience, proclaimed by black consciousness philosophy, was partially belied by events. The 1976 risings that cost over 600 lives as a result of police action marked the culmination of black consciousness as a political force and heralded its transformation.

The ideological assertion of the unity of the black experience was, ironically, being made at a time of growing divisions among blacks. The kinship system in the townships had in the past acted as an informal redistributive system; the family was a mini-welfare state rescuing unemployed and destitute kin from a humiliating and degrading poverty. But, as inflation sharpened, this solidarity was put under considerable strain between 1974 and 1976.

The major influx into the townships in the 1970s brought street crime and prostitution in areas like Soweto to epidemic proportions. Vast new shanty towns like those of the Winterveld region, only 35 km north of Pretoria, 80 km in diameter and with a population of over half a million, became some of the largest black towns in southern Africa. They spawned the full gamut of diseases associated with acute poverty, overcrowding and malnutrition. In urban conditions such as these, charity for the poor and education for the young, the traditional functions of the African family, became increasingly impossible for individual breadwinners.

Divisions and gross inequalities in wealth within the black

community have existed for a long time, but young blacks became increasingly aware of them. A new class of entrepreneurs grew up who dominated the so-called 'informal sector' and business enterprises in the townships, the owners of taxis, shebeens, prostitution rackets and, recently, chain-stores; some became well-known millionaires with political positions. The new political elites and landowners in the bantustans formed a different section of wealthy blacks who benefited from the economic basis of apartheid. Though few blacks are rural landlords, some in Winterveld earn rents from impoverished tenants and proceeds from water sales exceeding 600 Rand per week. Either coterminous with, or overarching, these differences in wealth were ethnic divisions equally sponsored by the South African government. It was against this background that black consciousness activists stimulated the formation of new political groupings like the Black People's Convention (BPC) and cemented together, as best they could, the black communities.

The informal residential segregation by income in black townships, the growing social stratification of the black community, and the dissemination of new magazines presenting an affluent black middle-class style of life drove increasingly politicised urban youth into an embryonic class analysis of the black predicament. Like their counterparts elsewhere, young people in the townships were particularly sensitive to life-style and ready to dismiss all those with above average housing or car and good education, as, in their words, 'not black', i.e. middle-class. This them-and-us perception within the black community began to bring into focus the importance of the black worker in political change during the development of the BCM in 1969-1976. This was reinforced by contact with African National Congress (ANC) members released after serving twelve-year sentences that began in the early 1960s after the Rivonia trial.

But beyond the social divisions created in the black community lies a more profound one of town versus 'homeland' with even more moral and political resonances. Unemployed blacks return to the rural areas only under considerable duress, because they are too old to continue, ill, or simply despair of finding work. Many born in town are forced into rural areas they have never seen before. In the last 15 years over 2 million people have been 'resettled' in 'homelands'. The return to the 'ethnic homeland' has thus become for many urban blacks the central moral issue; to go back to a bantustan has overtones of a betrayal of black pride and solidarity, the basic preoccupation of the Black Consciousness Movement. For this reason men like the leaders of the new 'independent states', Matanzima, Mangope and Mpephu, are seen by politicised urban blacks as outright traitors to the black cause. Chief Gatsha Buthelezi, who has refused 'independent' status for Kwazulu, while achieving celebrity from a homeland base, is strongly opposed both by those reared in a black consciousness tradition, and by those in the non-racial tradition that emerged in the UDF.

Class, Race and National Liberation

Government policy, especially since the advent of Mr P.W. Botha, is designed to reinforce divisions within the black community, indeed to accentuate them. On the other hand, the ANC, basing its programme of action on the 1955 Freedom Charter, has been strongly sponsoring a united black struggle involving all racial groups. During the same period, members of the Black Consciousness Movement have been meeting with leaders of the banned ANC, either during prison sentences, or in exile, after flight across the border in the wake of government repression. The ANC, which has followed a socialist analysis of South African society, and to which accrues the prestige of waging a growing guerrilla struggle, was therefore able to exert a renewed influence over young politicised blacks in the period 1977-1985. The Black Consciousness Movement thus found itself challenged by the longer established liberation movement and involved in a dialogue that has brought several waves of recruitment to the ranks of the ANC.

The abolition of all black consciousness affiliated organisations by the South African government in October 1977 forced large numbers of politicised urban blacks to leave the country, a position forced on the ANC and PAC (Pan-Africanist Congress), the two liberation movements recognised by the Organisation of African Unity, since the early 1960s. The experience of the BCM thus repeated, a generation later, that of the ANC and PAC. The 1977 bannings brought a new generation to the conclusion that non-violent, open, public methods of bringing about change were, at the time, impossible. When the Azanian People's Organisation (AZAPO) emerged briefly in May-June 1978, its BCM leadership was again rapidly eliminated by banning. AZAPO represented an amalgamation of black consciousness activists and members of the banned PAC. The latter had broken away from the ANC in 1959 for a variety of reasons; tactics, 'Indian' finance in the Congress Alliance and the role of a small group of largely white and 'Indian' communists, are often cited as the most important. In their shared distrust of white political involvement and their 'Africanist' stance, the PAC and Black Consciousness Movement had a similar outlook. However, after the death of the PAC leader, Robert Sobukwe, the

PAC leadership was left in great disarray, and several prominent members were imprisoned in Swaziland during 1978-1979. Major regrouping is now taking place though the organisation has suffered an irreversible loss of prestige.

The breakdown of PAC organisation and BCM's growing dialogue with the ANC meant that when black consciousness activists regrouped in September 1979 to reform AZAPO the new group immediately engaged in a debate on the role of the black worker and on non-collaborationist tactics towards the government. The 1979 AZAPO, more so than the 1978 grouping, thus appeared initially to represent a transitional stage in the evolution of the Black Consciousness Movement in the direction of the ANC analysis of society. Two positions, 'All blacks are workers', requiring the exclusion of whites, versus a rigorous non-racial class analysis, were in conflict within AZAPO. This conflict lay behind the early suspension of the AZAPO leader, Curtis Nkondo, who later became prominent in the UDF. The result of these debates has been an increasingly sophisticated analysis of the black predicament along Marxist lines within the BCM tradition, and a greater emphasis on direct political engagement than the former community programmes.

Though there are a few who would wish the Black Consciousness Movement to develop as a 'third way' solution to South African nationalism, for the majority of politicised blacks the BCM has been an historic — and necessary — stage in the growth of black political consciousness. Since the ANC remains banned in South Africa while AZAPO has survived — in the space created by Mr P.W. Botha's attempts to convince western investors of the reality of change — movements growing out of a BCM tradition will continue to play a role in the 1980s. Local sources suggest that this role is increasingly becoming that of a 'Trotskyite' rival to the ANC and a forum for black rejection of white participation in the liberation struggle. The creation in May 1983 of a National Forum Committee, apparently a counter grouping to the non-racial United Democratic Front, was a striking example of the direction of this approach. The fundamental defect of AZAPO, lack of support from workers, unemployed and 'homelands' residents, plus organisational difficulties created by surveillance and state control over meetings, places limits on its independent growth.

Similar ambiguities and problems at first beset the Soweto Civic Association with its older and more affluent membership. Led by national figures of the stature of Dr Nthato Motlana and Bishop Desmond Tutu, with strong roots in the black theology of the 1970s, the association grew out of the 'Committee of Ten' at the end of 1979. The association retained the essential black consciousness style of non-collaboration and protest politics, and therefore found itself repeatedly at loggerheads with Chief Gatsha Buthelezi. Dialogue with new members and student activists has led them into the UDF.

Civic, tenants' and residents' associations, often with a community newspaper, have prospered in a number of cities and townships, organising around such issues as rising rents and bus fares, the provision of electricity, and state moves to sell municipally owned houses to their 'coloured' and 'Indian' occupants. The possibilities of the new civic associations are directly correlated with their ability to call up support from black blue-collar workers, a point much debated by AZAPO. They have proved particularly effective in organising consumer boycotts of white shops, buses and other targets selected by the community in the Eastern Cape. The forging of links between trades union and black community politics is likely to remain pivotal in the future. Equally, such movements depend on the support of young people in urban areas, whose judgements can be severe on those falling into the carefully laid traps of the Botha government, and whose response to those breaking boycotts is often harsh.

The main youth organisation, the Congress of South African Students, COSAS, has been able to direct school pupils in their boycott campaigns and in pressure for student representative councils in schools. Following a non-racial strategy, they have been highly effective in mobilising young people both on the streets and in the classroom. Their analysis of South Africa is now shared with AZASO, the Azanian Student Organisation and by the majority of Youth Congresses, the community-based youth groups which emerged between 1983 and 1985. Together these youth groups have been the cutting edge of black resistance, drawing in parents, linking with trades unionists and civic associations and risking their lives on the streets and in detention. The banning of COSAS in August 1985 was a tacit admission by the state of their success. To counter their immense influence AZAPO created its own youth wing, AZASM, the Azanian Students' Movement, which has limited influence, mainly in the Transvaal.

Although the movements growing out of the BCM tradition only have significant influence in Soweto and Cape Town, and this greatly diminished by splits, they are often put forward as rivals to the UDF and to the ANC. But to put the small AZAPO membership against the vast national support for UDF and the ANC is to give a very distorted picture of black resistance. There is little doubt that the violent rivalry that grew up in early 1985 between UDF affiliates and AZAPO has been damaging, and was played on by the state to good effect, but ultimately it is unlikely to divert the liberation struggle. At the same time the state of emergency has thrown together old ideological opponents and consolidated black unity; the *Kairos Document*, for example, gained assent from theologians on both sides of this divide.

The United Democratic Front (UDF)

The formation in August 1983, after six months of preparation, of a national, non-racial United Democratic Front against Mr P.W. Botha's constitutional proposals was a tangible sign of the broad black consensus for genuine democracy. The UDF is an umbrella organisation consisting of some 650 groups, including civic associations, Christian and Islamic groups, trade unions, women's organisations and sporting and cultural bodies. It represents the greatest upsurge in black politics since the Congress movement of the early 1950s.

The strength of the opposition it organised to the constitutional proposals and the success of its subsequent campaign for a boycott of the structures of the tri-cameral parliament were testimony both to its vigour and to the seeds sown in generations of black resistance to apartheid. The challenge now facing it is to create a viable grass-roots organisation that will survive government detention of its outstanding national leadership. This demands a leadership at all levels capable of moving beyond mobilisation around particular issues to a sustained political involvement through mass movements, a slow and daunting task.

The state's attempt to crush the UDF has taken a number of different forms: treason trials of its leadership to eliminate them from political life, repeated raids on UDF offices, banning of the Congress of South African Students, COSAS, one of its most effective youth affiliates, and state of emergency provisions that stop all meetings except those defined narrowly as 'religious'. With most of the UDF's leaders either in prison or in hiding, the task of organisation demands new skills, new methods and a high level of discipline amongst its members.

It would be foolish, therefore, to pretend that black resistance had not suffered a setback from the imposition of the state of emergency. Organisation has become extremely difficult as leaders of the legal non-racial movement are forced to work in hiding from the security police. The UDF was not intended as an underground organisation and it has been obliged to find new ways of organising under the current repression. But against these temporary setbacks stands the tremendous gain of an unprecedented mobilisation of the black community as a result of the state's brutal tactics. This mobilisation now includes whole 'coloured' communities around Cape Town, small townships in the Orange Free State, formerly apolitical Christian and Muslim groups, as well as UDF's previous large constituency, which is holding firm.

However with over half the UDF's office-bearers arrested, on trial for high treason or murdered, it will become difficult for it to resist the criminalisation of its democratic activities that the state is seeking. A major trial of 22 UDF-linked detainees (the Delmas 22) begins in 1986. Instructively it was the four SAAWU trades unionists among the Pietermaritzburg UDF 12 who did not have treason charges against them dropped, and will also be standing trial. UDF-affiliated organisations have not always worked harmoniously with trades unions, and the state seeks to sponsor division.

Many of the ideological and practical differences that appeared significant during the relative freedom to organise of the period 1980-1985 appear much less so to organisations on the run. Practical problems of pursuing campaigns and sheer survival are displacing ideological conflicts. The UDF remains a legal, non-racial organisation, committed to non-violent forms of struggle. Active membership of the UDF is now treated by the state *de facto* as a criminal act so that leaders who have been released from detention or who are emerging from hiding live in constant fear of the early morning knock on the door. In a remarkably short time, through united action and the resulting repression of white activists in affiliated organisations, like the Johannesburg Democratic Action Committee (JODAC), it has shown the possibilities for a future free South Africa.

Inkatha

Although the principal enemy of both AZAPO and the UDF is apartheid, a significant secondary one has emerged in Inkatha, the Zulu Cultural Association launched as a movement in 1975 by Chief Gatsha Buthelezi. Grown into a powerful political party that dominates the life of KwaZulu, Inkatha, claims about a million card-carrying members and, with support amongst Zulu speakers in Soweto, is in practice the largest internal political association legally available to blacks within South Africa.* It has, however, until now followed a policy of dialogue and collaboration in strong contrast to the protest politics and non-collaboration of groups in the BCM and non-racial traditions.

The power of Inkatha in Natal is best compared to that of the Malawi Congress Party in newly independent Nyasaland two decades ago. It rests heavily on the political skills of its leader, Chief

---

*The UDF, though theoretically legal, like SACTU, is treated as illegal.

Buthelezi, who does not suffer intellectual rivals easily. Autocratic leadership has created far from unequivocal support amongst the party's intelligentsia. Possession of the three-Rand party card is more than helpful for successful dealings with KwaZulu authorities, and business life without it in Natal can be difficult for blacks. Nominal membership is thus a deceptive guide to real support, given the current climate of violent coercion reported by observers in KwaZulu. A women's and youth league play an important role in the life of the region, while Inkatha's coercive control of the 'homeland's' life, schools and business has brought it into conflict with the churches.

Nonetheless Chief Buthelezi was once able to count on crowds of 10,000-20,000 for his speeches in Soweto — not all, of course, residents of Soweto — and once reached a sizeable public through his paper, *The Nation*. In distinction to the growing socialist emphasis of the new BCM groups, he has maintained a canny public stance, being prepared to co-operate indiscriminately with large corporations to obtain investment in KwaZulu. His past willingness to let Inkatha stand for the despised community councils in the townships and to participate in frequent discussions with government leaders has given him a purchase on what little political life is available to blacks outside the context of 'independent states'. His refusal to accept 'independence' for KwaZulu has cost him little, and remains the central plank of his support amongst educated Zulu-speakers, who contrast him with the Quisling leaders of the 'independent homelands'. His astute political tightrope walk once enabled him to call on the prestige of a past close association with the ANC leadership while repeatedly repudiating armed struggle as a means of liberating South Africa.

Many see Buthelezi's problem as that of a man pulling himself up by his bootstraps. The KwaZulu government and Inkatha are virtually synonymous. The party teaches its programmes in KwaZulu schools, it runs public services and buses, so that popular resistance to 'the state' has inevitably brought protesters into conflict with Inkatha. Inkatha lacks a strong voice in the important Durban-based unions and urban youth in Durban townships like Kwamashu, Umlazi and Lamontville. Its stance as custodian of 'law and order' during the school boycotts of April-July 1980, the use of strong-arm men against students, calls for vigilantes to protect property, and references to ANC agitators thoroughly alienated politicised young people.

The role of Inkatha in relation to democratic organisations became increasingly threatening after the launch of the UDF, which it saw as a challenge. Chief Buthelezi's national stature, maintained by constant wide press coverage, and considerable foreign financial support, has degenerated to a point where the ANC took the unprecedented step of engaging in a strong and public denunciation of his tactics, thereby reversing a policy of not criticising internal political groups.

Inkatha's role in the liberation struggle had been helpfully set out in the 1982 report of the Buthelezi Commission:

'Popular sentiments appear to be such as to create a climate which will encourage, justify and protect groups aiming at creating instability in the country. While a revolutionary situation has not yet emerged in general terms within the population inside South Africa, developments appear to point in that direction. The importance of legitimate internal Black political organisations like Inkatha and others in directing Black South African political sentiments along *peaceful and constructive lines* cannot be overemphasised' (Italics added).

After that time, COSAS was banned in KwaZulu schools, where students are automatically registered as Inkatha members by their principals, who pay a one-Rand fee for each pupil. A year later, Inkatha's 'peaceful and constructive' approach brought death to four students and injury to 113 at the hands of a Zulu *impi*, a band of thugs, at the University of Zululand. Inkatha's violent tactics have been deliberately ignored by its business allies because of its opposition, since 1980, to the ANC, to democratic organisations and trades unions in South Africa, and particularly because of Chief Buthelezi's championing of opposition to economic sanctions. The business world's control of the mass media can be seen in the successful propaganda portrayal of Chief Buthelezi as the 'moderate' proponent of peaceful change, the 'internal' leader set against the 'external' ANC.

The dramatic increase of support for the ANC and the rapid rise of the non-racial UDF exposed the contradictions in Chief Buthelezi's position and revealed the political nature of Inkatha more clearly. Its essential features combine the claim to a radical political tradition, cultural roots and support amongst rural people in Natal, with groups of thugs forcing people to become members and opposition to socialist unions, giving the movement an attraction to the business community, who believe they can work with it.

The period 1980-1985 saw Inkatha become an ethnic battering ram manipulated by powerful interests outside itself. The rise of democratic organisations in the last two years, popular attacks on collaborationist groups, and, finally, the state of emergency, have now thrust Inkatha to the centre of the stage in Natal as an important, if unwitting, arm of the apartheid system. The instances of police-Inkatha collusion in the repression of the UDF and Chief Buthelezi's role in the Western debate on economic sanctions should have been sufficient to remove any doubts which still lingered. The last six months have raised the frightening spectre of an authoritarian movement bringing civil war to a South Africa in transition to majority rule.

The Durban riots

During the first week of August 1985, 70 people died in fighting and rioting, 43 were killed by the police and over 200 were badly injured in the Durban area. The exact causes of the riots that devastated parts of the predominantly Indian area of Inanda and Phoenix township were difficult to clarify in the overall confusion. It was not, as the press portrayed it, a simple Indian-African racial riot. Both African and Indian shops were burnt to the ground. African families housed fleeing Indians and vice versa. It did demonstrate, however, how quickly political protest can get out of hand, and reinforced the growing realisation in the non-racial movement that it still has a long way to go in organising and conscientising communities.

The murder on 1 August of Victoria Mxenge, a prominent Civil Rights lawyer, member of the UDF and Release Mandela Campaign, and revered community leader in Umlazi, sparked the unrest. The weekend after her murder by four armed men, youth groups planned boycotts of schools in protest and began blocking roads into Indian areas, apparently in preparation for a wider stay-away. Attacks on shops that stayed open and refused to close in mourning, and on areas of known support for the collaborationist National People's Party, appear to have spilled over into indiscriminate looting of empty Indian property vacated by frightened families. Despite repeated appeals, police refused to take any action so Indian families began to evacuate their homes.

The situation might easily have been brought under control had not police and security forces had a vested interest in seeing it simmer. It was only on 7 August, three days after trouble had started, that the situation got out of hand, largely because of the intervention of Inkatha. According to eyewitnesses, a crowd of 5,000 attending a peaceful memorial service in Umlazi Arena were attacked by a Zulu *impi* of 300, ushered in by police. Fifteen people were killed in the resulting fracas, in which sticks and spears were used. This attack heralded the arrival of other Zulu *impi* in Malagasi, Kwamashu and Lamontville. Anti-UDF mobs roamed the townships attacking suspected supporters and young people. On 9 August a group of 1,000 marched through Kwamashu in a show of strength against the UDF. In other incidents, fighting broke out at the Phoenix Mahatma Gandhi Centre, where UDF refugees from Hambanathi were staying. The centre was devastated. Indian vigilantes began patrolling Inanda and Phoenix owing to the absence of police and security forces.

The Durban riots provided Inkatha with the pretext it required to engage in a crusade against the UDF. There is now enough evidence indicating deliberate provocation of black communities by Security Police to suggest that this might have been the motivation behind the murder of Victoria Mxenge.

Since the riots, Inkatha's role in relation to the business world and the state has been graphically illustrated. At Imbali where a longstanding dispute between 1,000 workers and a SARMCOL factory began in April 1985, with church support for the workers, Inkatha has been terrorising the Imbali Civic Association, Youth Organisation and members of the Midlands UDF. A member of COSAS was murdered but the police have maintained a calculated distance. At a meeting in the Imbali Community Hall on 25 August, the KwaZulu MP, Mr V.B. Ndlovu, called on the armed audience to be rid of the Federal Seminary, which he accused of fomenting disorder and harbouring criminals. (The UDF 16 had been spending their nights there during their trial for high treason.) About one hundred armed men then approached the seminary, and threatened to close it down. A High Court action restraining Inkatha from attacking the Federal Seminary had to be sought. A day later, Mr Paddy Kearney, director of the ecumenical centre, Diakonia, was detained by security police; the centre supported the SARMCOL workers and was seen by Chief Buthelezi as an important support for UDF. On 27 August Rev Mcebisi Xundu, who had spearheaded opposition to Lamontville's incorporation into KwaZulu, was detained under Section 29 of the Internal Security Act. During the Durban riots, a mob had sought out the retiring chairman of Diakonia, Rev Wesley Mabuza, a Methodist minister, humiliated him and forced him to sing anti-UDF songs. Early in September Thabo Mokoena, a member of the UDF-affiliated National Federation of Workers, was beaten to death by a gang of 20 men after being abducted from his home. Such killings and assaults have continued.

Chief Buthelezi is therefore an important card in the hand of the white power bloc, but a potentially difficult one to play in the current game of 'power sharing' formulas. On the one hand, while his support among urban blacks is indicated by surveys to be under 8%, he can deliver an important active black constituency of perhaps half a million, mainly rural, Zulu speakers. This contrasts favourably with the minimal support enjoyed by the co-opted 'coloured' and 'Indian' ministers, in their communities. On the other hand, the violence of Inkatha is rapidly alienating young people in the townships and the Chief's autocratic style of leadership is ill-suited to democratic township politics. Similarly the 'reform' strategy of extending civil rights to wider circles of citizens does not rest easily with rule by Zulu *impi*.

Inkatha, in its many roles, spans the splits in the white power bloc

48

but may therefore suffer as they become more acute. The convention politics of the transnationals and big business now seeks negotiations and deals. Change is projected as coming through different leaders being brought into a negotiating process and 'reforms' being instituted by enlightened leadership. The Afrikaner right wants repression. However, the transnationals' formula is no less redolent of bloodshed. As leaders have been co-opted into the laager, since the introduction of the new constitution in 1983, violence has grown immeasurably. The present attempt to co-opt Inkatha threatens a far more violent future as Zulu *impi* fight against democratic organisations. South Africa finds itself on the verge of civil war because of a policy of change from the top. Convention politics offers more of the same, though worse. Black South Africa does not want to be co-opted and accommodated in the violence of the apartheid system. It wants the system dismantled. The strategy of the state, directed by Mr P.W. Botha or by a more astute successor, founders on this reality today as it will tomorrow. The Inkatha uniform, imitating the colours of the ANC, now evokes the same fears as that of the police and army amongst leaders of democratic black resistance. It is the last black card in the state's pack.

ANC Ascendant

Inkatha's eagerness to don the colours of the ANC stems from the Congress's historic role as the senior liberation movement of South Africa. Founded in 1912 and the architect of the famous 1955 Freedom Charter, it gained a new lease of life after the 1976 risings. Internationally recognised, with numerous underground cells in certain major South African cities and industrial areas, and a military wing that has stepped up attacks on urban areas in the last few years, the ANC maintains a traditional authority in black nationalism. Wedded to a strong non-racialism and therefore intellectually opposed to the black exclusivism that characterised the old BCM, the ANC gained important new young recruits in the wake of the 1976 police riots. No other movement is as geared to benefit from the labour militancy and student protest that now dominate black politics. Similarly, in its central policy statement, the Freedom Charter, the ANC puts forward a programme for the whole nation, appealing to a wide spectrum of opinion in its emphasis on democracy and egalitarianism.

But though the ANC is experiencing a rejuvenating influx of new supporters from South Africa's townships, and has maintained its traditional structure as an umbrella organisation containing a nationalist spectrum from Africanist to Marxist, its Moscow-linked image persists in the South African media. This is largely because the South African government successfully portrays the ANC for propaganda purposes as nothing but a front organisation for the South African Communist Party (SACP). Government sources are not slow to attribute military action within the country to the ANC, giving a picture of terrorist activity by white communists directed from Moscow. This propaganda device reassures white South Africans in the categories of government ideology, and at the same time casts the nationalist struggle in Cold War terms appealing to conservatives in the West. On the other hand, the contribution of SACP members within the ANC has undeniably been significant. Of the different elements within the Congress, which includes many Christians, some ordained ministers, and some Moslems, the communists have, in the past, been the most disciplined, closely-knit and able to make their strategies prevail. The mutual influence exerted between the ANC and SACP has been historically important and lies behind the generally non-empirical Marxist literature produced by the Congress, as well as its strict party discipline. These were some of the factors which precluded any dramatic coming together of re-emergent BCM groups in exile with the ANC, a possibility worked against by the South African government, which nurtures the communist image of the ANC, and sought after by BCM leaders Steve Biko and Barney Pityana. Instead, many rank-and-file and some prominent members of the BCM have joined ANC individually.

The socialist analysis of society favoured by the ANC gives it strong support amongst black workers in certain key industrial areas. The strikes and boycotts of June/August 1980, for example, were concentrated in the Eastern Cape motor-car industry and schools, where the ANC has always been strong. In the Eastern Cape this tradition has formed the basis for a strong, dynamic ANC leadership in the townships, and high levels of local organisation. This has been fed by redundant workers. The growing appreciation by black workers of the strength of organised labour, coupled with the effects of economic recession in creating unemployment and reducing state services, is likely to increase the political content of strikes.

In the economic recession, retrenched politicised workers are likely, with nothing to gain and overshadowed by the spectre of homelands poverty, to turn increasingly to the national liberation struggle in underground activity. The military wing of the ANC, despite its lack of proper bases in countries bordering South Africa, seems to have impressed young urban blacks by its frequent attacks on symbols of white rule. The major successful operations of the early 1980s, particularly the spectacular attack on the Sasolburg oil installations and the Koeberg nuclear plant, produced widespread rejoicing in black townships. Even the devastating bomb blast in central Pretoria in May 1983 was welcomed by the majority of blacks despite heavy black casualties. A growing number see the ANC's military wing, Umkhonto we Sizwe, as a 'People's Army' and give it support and encouragement. This has had, together with the success of ZANLA in Zimbabwe, the effect of encouraging advocates of an expanded guerrilla war in the councils of the ANC, and aiding recruitment to the military wing. There is, however, a widespread recognition that guerrilla war will play a very different role from its part in the liberation struggles in Zimbabwe, Mozambique and Angola. This is partly a reflection of the different structures of South African society, its urban, industrial base. South Africa's ruthless destabilisation of neighbouring states has also made the presence even of South African refugees in them potentially a costly liability.

After the deaths of its citizens in South African raids, Lesotho was obliged to comply with South Africa's demands or face economic ruin; South African refugees agreed to leave. More followed from Swaziland, Botswana and Mozambique under similar pressures. A Maseru resident, asked if he was pleased to be rid of the South African refugees, expressed an opinion that illustrates the wider plight of the Frontline states. 'No, this is just the beginning. The Boers will find other ways to humiliate us.' In early 1984 the Nkomati and Lusaka accords, denying ANC troops passage through the Frontline states in South Africa, demonstrated the wisdom of his remark. Nevertheless within a year bombs were going off again in South African cities at the rate of almost one a day, as the ANC began military training within the townships. 122 armed attacks were counted by Pretoria's Institute of Strategic Studies in the year to mid-December 1985, triple the 1984 figure. There were also major attacks on South Africa's coal to oil plants at Secunda, and land mines were planted in northern Transvaal.

The ANC thus confronts the future with strange ironies. With perhaps never so much broad support in South Africa — certainly an urban electoral majority, according to opinion polls — its regional position has suffered setbacks. The fact that the ANC's analysis of Nkomati proved correct, and that of Samora Machel tragically wrong, is little consolation. The Frontline states, through necessity, cannot afford the ANC substantial help, least of all tangible military support. The West's relation to the ANC is particularly confused. The British Government has called for the unconditional release of Nelson Mandela, whether or not he renounces violence, but refuses to talk to the ANC while it supports violence. The diplomatic and humanitarian support of the Scandinavian countries, Netherlands and Austria contrasts sharply with the problems faced by the ANC in relations with Britain.

These are some of the influences that resulted in an important call by the National Executive of the ANC in early May 1985 to all South Africans, broadcast on Addis Ababa's Radio Freedom, and reproduced inside South Africa. In it the ANC responded to the unique character of the urban revolt with an unprecedented demand for the people to seize the opportunity created by the collapse of township government. Underground groups, 'small mobile units which will protect the people . . . and act in an organised way' were called for. Such groups would work alongside regular ANC troops and attempt to build up supplies of arms, captured or made, that would enable them to engage security forces. The ANC statement wanted the vacuum in the townships filled with popular organisations able to take control. Though interpreted as a call for a popular uprising, the statement seemed to follow logically from the policy of expanding the liberation struggle into a 'people's war', from the need felt in the townships for protection against the police.

The call was followed a month later by the first consultative conference of the ANC since 1969, held in Zambia. It reinforced the ANC's non-racial philosophy with the first non-African appointments to the executive and confirmed its commitment to widen the armed struggle through a 'people's war' to make South Africa ungovernable. Following calls to unity and an end to strife between BCM groups and UDF groups, it presented the black consciousness movement as a progressive step in the history of black resistance while rejecting out of hand the pretentions of Inkatha. At the same time it emphasised its concern for the development of worker leadership in the liberation struggle, reflecting the powerful voice of the black worker movement in the country.

The ANC is thus now mounting a multi-pronged campaign, giving growing emphasis to armed struggle, worker organisation and the creation of a resilient internal movement. The ANC-allied trades union federation, SACTU, has correspondingly benefited from years of underground work by a small core of active shop stewards, and public education work by radical unionists. Thus the Congress, while stressing the flexible, democratic principles of its Freedom Charter, finds itself today a strictly disciplined underground movement with a wide penumbra of sympathisers making preparations for an expanded guerrilla war, a position it assumed in the face of the intransigence of the South African government, after pursuing a policy of non-violent change for half a century. It is safe to say that, in all political or social groupings and associations, ANC members and sympathisers will be found pressing for a worker orientation and pushing debate into the context of national liberation. While a small minority will be committed communists, many more will seek a nationalism involving varying degrees of socialist transformation of society coupled with a strong element of state control.

52

The Radicalisation of Black Nationalism

Since the Soweto riots of 1976 the oppression of blacks, apartheid and capitalism have become virtually synonymous for many blacks, irrespective of their nominal political affiliation. For some this equation has worked out as a complete rejection of both the West and Western Christianity. The success of the guerrilla wars in Mozambique and Zimbabwe has left them with little doubt of the advisability of armed struggle. Debates about the merits of violent as against non-violent change, communism as against democracy, rarely preoccupy politically active blacks. The importance these issues assume in European and North American discussions is frequently regarded as a confirmation of Western distance from the black predicament, if not, in the Marxist language which is becoming increasingly common, as an ideological expression of 'imperialism'. Blacks' experience in the South Africa of the last decade has defined the struggle of the next decade irreversibly as one for a socialist transformation of society, partly by military means. It would be foolish to analyse the cautiously modulated speeches of black leaders, alert to the strict constraints of the national security state, for evidence to the contrary. Black South Africa has been forced 'underground'; what appears on the surface in the white apartheid desert is artfully adapted to needs and conditions. What appears at township funerals is a revolutionary ferment led by young people that bodes ill for big business. It was precisely this realisation that sent representatives of the business community to Lusaka in October 1985 in a bid to safeguard their investments for the future.

The Independent Black Unions

The radicalisation of black nationalism has had as an important component the growing power of black workers through union organisation. In 1982 the level of strike activity was double that of 1973 during the massive Durban-based strikes, and the duration and intensity of the activity has remained a testimony to a growing solidarity between black workers. This represents more than a narrow quest for purely economic gain, and expresses an identity that is more than an introverted solidarity between those who have jobs.

In the face of the stiff penalty of sacking followed by forced removal to impoverished 'homelands', workers have staged strikes against both retrenchment and unfair dismissal. A massive one-day protest marked the death in detention of Neil Aggett. Trades unions in 1981 opposed the granting of 'independence' to Ciskei and staged a massive political strike in November 1984 against the military occupation of the townships. So it would be, to date, a false opposition to set this new worker consciousness against action for national liberation on the ground that elsewhere, for example in the West, many unions have forsaken political goals and become sectarian pressure groups believing in little but economic advantage. In December the general secretary of the new trade union federation, COSATU, met the ANC in Lusaka. The ANC welcomed the formation of COSATU; COSATU described the meeting as fruitful, and both agreed that COSATU is an independent organisation, democratically accountable to its members.

The rise of the black independent trades union movement has therefore been heralded by the international community, church leaders and Marxist theorists alike as a turning point in the liberation of South Africa. Arising out of the advice centres, workers' legal aid and training projects of the early 1970s, a decade later the union movement has surged into militant opposition to racial capitalism. Until the world recession brought some retrenchment, illegal black strikes were growing almost exponentially, drawing in increasing numbers of workers. By 1986, the proportion of workers in unions was approaching the level of some industrial states; some key sectors, notably railways, remained unorganised, but in others, such as metals, unions had a decisive following. This growth has opened up expectations that the worker movement would become a dominant political force.

A decade of union organisation produced three major union groupings. FOSATU was a federation including a wide range of unions with varied approaches towards registration with the state, joining industrial councils and taking up extra-workplace issues; through its constituent organisations it combined a non-racial organisation with solid shop-floor unionism. CUSA is a smaller federation which grew out of the black consciousness rejection of radical white trade unionists; it is heavily funded from abroad, with a consequent tendency to produce over-powerful general secretaries. There is also a great variety of independent militant unions, Food and Canning Workers, GAWU, SAAWU, and GWU, a union originally confined to the Western Cape. All these have experienced rapid expansion and a wave of popularity in the last five years. None grew faster than the National Union of Mineworkers (NUM) in the critical coal, gold and diamond industries; it had gained over 120,000 members by late 1985.

Differences over tactics, and sheer competitiveness among union leaders, meant that a united union movement appeared a distant goal until 1985. Government and transnationals have also tried to control the unions through Wiehahn structures and by either co-opting or repressing union leaders. These tactics have fostered divisions within the movement. There have been differences on such questions as the need for general rather than industrial unions, and relationships with student and civic organisations. Under these lay two major issues: how were the unions in the short term to maximise gains for the small percentage of labour that was unionised and how, in the long term, were they as worker organisations to contribute to the wider movement for national liberation?

Unions have the potential to paralyse the apartheid system; the NUM, for example, has already achieved impressive increases in wage levels after a major strike that split the powerful Chamber of Mines. The white power bloc is, without doubt, aware and frightened of this potential.

The repression of trade unionists making 'political demands' — the standard government description for union discussion even of issues such as housing and pensions — heightened debate within the federations. Some feared that any deviation from a narrow definition of trade union activity would result in a violent reaction from the state. Others, primarily the non-registered unions, were prepared to take the risk, balancing the strong popular support for radical demands against the resulting mushroom growth which strained the unions' organisational resources. The result was one of the most thoughtful, yet militant, trade union movements in the world, weighing up the formidable task of confronting both state and transnationals through the depression of the mid-1980s.

The maturity of the black union movement was demonstrated by its ability to overcome the considerable differences in approach within it to create a powerful new super-federation drawing in FOSATU, NUM, GWU, Food and Canning, and unions that had affiliated to the UDF like SAAWU and GAWU, virtually all the independent 'non-racial' unions. CUSA remained outside, as did AZACTU, a tiny union group spawned by AZAPO. 34 unions signed an agreement in November 1985 to form COSATU, the Congress of South African Trade Unions. Though many difficulties remain to be overcome, the new federation will represent the largest number of black unionised workers ever in the history of South Africa. Led by an NUM President with a general secretary drawn from the former FOSATU affiliate, the militant Sweet, Food and Allied Workers Union, COSATU will be a powerful political force.

There is every indication that in South Africa workers' nationalism, their demands for political rights, cannot be achieved under the prevailing system of racial capitalism. Far from being co-opted under the Wiehahn strategy, unions have become increasingly militant and unwilling to comply with the demands of state control. The COSATU leaders have immediately set down strong political demands, threatened to burn passes, endorsed sanctions, and called for troops to leave the townships. The current recession and state repression, which may curb this militancy, will also certainly harden the attitude of management, giving workers further cause to identify their interests firmly with opposition to racial capitalism. With the return of retrenched workers to the homelands, and growing class consciousness and experience among black union leaders, it seems likely that the direction of the internal movement of the African National Congress will increasingly be dominated by worker perceptions of the South African system.

While, owing to the industrialised nature of the South African economy, everything points to the pivotal role of black workers in any future overthrow of the apartheid system, the radicalisation of black workers is far from complete. For agricultural labourers, for example, it has scarcely begun and in some areas of Natal Inkatha has been divisive. Nevertheless the trades union movement is likely to remain throughout the 1980s a vital sector in the struggle for South Africa.

The Middle Class

Militancy is not, of course, the prerogative of black workers alone. Despite the concessions planned for a black middle class, the BCM and the UDF, combined with government repression, have created in this middle class a highly politicised group that will be satisfied with nothing less than their full civil and political rights within a unified South Africa. Police and military brutality among the 'coloured' and 'Indian' communities has put paid to any prospect of their co-option. The acquiescence of the Coloured Labour Party in the 1983 constitution was met by a widespread boycott of elections by the 'coloured' community. At the same time a normally quiescent 'Indian' community has been partially politicised, with the formation of a Transvaal Indian Congress and the resurgence of the Natal Indian Congress.

The independence of Zimbabwe following seven years of armed struggle fuelled expectations. After the widespread rejoicing at ZANU (PF)'s victory among those in South Africa most often branded as 'middle-class', the chances of the South African government's finding significant collaborationist groups like Bishop Muzorewa's UANC now seem slim. At the most, the ethnic support for Inkatha will be further mobilised as a battering ram against the liberation movement. Attempts to set the ANC in conflict with other groups through foreign interference or South African propaganda seem equally idle at present. The campaign to free the ANC leader, Nelson Mandela, is being sponsored by men like Mr Percy Qoboza and Bishop Desmond Tutu, both pillars of the Soweto establishment. While it is true that the South African government does try to 'divide and rule' black political groups, the Release Mandela Campaign, calling for the release of a man capable of unifying black political opinion, demonstrates how aware the black community remains of such tactics.

The Future

The South African government's attempts to maintain and remodel their apartheid groundplan, advocated two decades ago by Afrikaner strategists, have had the unforeseen consequences of eliciting uncontrollable black revolt in the townships. The meteoric rise of the UDF from August 1983 until the state crack-down in February 1985 demonstrated a depth of resistance that could not be broken by repression. By the end of 1985 Muslims were firing at police from Cape mosques. Christians were defining apartheid government as tyranny, that is, illegitimate, and in parts of the Eastern Cape township residents had taken control of their townships. Troops appeared in numbers as an army of occupation, while the police force was augmented and integrated as the repressive arm of white rule. Rents and service bills remained unpaid in many townships and, overall, young people behaved like the 'people's army' they were summoned to create by the ANC.

Trades unions are gaining ground and showing a strong political commitment to national liberation. The black middle class shows few signs of being ready to be bought off with concessions that are too little and too late. An increasing number of young people also seem willing to face shut-down schools and great personal danger, seeing no future other than the one their sacrifices may make possible. In the final analysis the South African government is faced with two alternatives: a rapid movement to majority rule under genuine black leaders like Nelson Mandela, with all that this implies for government and society, or an unprecedented level of repression.

The tide of black nationalism is beginning to sweep away possibilities for any middle way in which some relaxation at the centre for urban residents could be paid for by growing repression and impoverishment at the periphery. Mr Botha's historic 'compromise' has fallen apart. His National Party majority is being

57

eroded heavily on the right after the defection of the Conservative Party. The government's attempts to move from racial to liberal capitalist structures has encountered a major stumbling block, allowing black resistance to consolidate. The immediate future, however, is dominated by the possibility of the release of Nelson Mandela. His release would be a tremendous achievement, primarily for the democratic groups inside South Africa who have made it a cornerstone of their demands, but also for international pressure. Mr Botha's usual talk of 'reforms' involves amending apartheid from above, some day, after graciously consulting those he accepts as black leaders. Releasing Mandela is the first step on the alternative path put forward by the ANC and the UDF, a path which leads through the release of all political prisoners and the unbanning of political organisations to the abolition of apartheid, negotiation for the transfer of power and one person, one vote in a unitary South Africa.

But the significance of Mandela's release if it occurs, should not be exaggerated. There is no indication that the South African government intends to go down this alternative path. No other political prisoners are involved in the negotiations. The release of SWAPO leader Toivo Ja Toivo in 1984 did not lead to progress towards freedom for Namibia; the trend has been, if anything, in the opposite direction. Without further steps down the alternative path, South Africa will remain on the course euphemistically called 'violent equilibrium', in other words, a prolonged war of national liberation.

Conclusions

For a number of different reasons the South African black struggle for political rights and social justice in the 1980s will be unique in the history of Africa. Firstly, the process is not, as in other African countries, one of decolonisation susceptible to resolution by imperial metropolitan powers. Although there is a widespread sense of 'us next' in South Africa, the last *colonial* domino is Namibia rather than the Republic. As a result the coming civil war in South Africa is likely to be unprecedented in its ferocity, extent and consequences for world peace. The devastating urban rioting and state violence and South Africa's repeated violations of its neighbours' territorial sovereignty are signs of the gathering storm in southern Africa.

There are no readily available models for a transfer of power in South Africa. Independence and the subsequent transformation, or stagnation, of local economies in the other states of Southern Africa, have been profoundly influenced by the economic might of the Republic. This important 'governor' controlling the pace of change will, of course, be missing from the constraints on any black majority government in South Africa itself.

Secondly, the South African nationalist movement has important characteristics that were largely lacking from Africa's other nationalist movements. There has been almost a century of articulate black political struggle for freedom and some 60 years of socialist influence on black nationalism. From 1948, when the National Party of the Afrikaners came to power, until today, the peculiar deformities of apartheid have driven black worker and black middle class into a dialogue about economic exploitation. Since 1976 this dialogue, sponsored by the ANC, has produced a broad consensus against capitalism, and in favour of armed struggle. Intellectuals, students, and professionals have persistently been driven back amongst the black working class as ladders of social mobility were kicked away by apartheid policies. There they met natural working class leaders whose challenge, and the challenge of politicised youth, had repeatedly to be answered to assure political credibility. By the 1980s apartheid had created an intellectual vanguard to an unprecedently large and alienated working class, the formula for a revolutionary party. Provided that this vanguard does not degenerate into an academic ultra-left sect, such a revolutionary party is likely to collect widespread support in the black community in the coming decade.

Whatever happens to black nationalism, two things are sure. Endowed with one of the most sophisticated leaderships of any African nationalist movement, South African blacks will be neither politically naive nor slow to identify their friends in the world community. And they will not find themselves, as other states have done under the shadow of South Africa, hostage in quite the same way to the interests of the international business community.

While it is understandable that the Western world imagines it can temper its moral scruples about apartheid with the pragmatism of its strategic interests, this may be a very short-sighted vision. The West has avoided choosing between South Africa and the rest of the continent in the first years of the 1980s, but it becomes less and less possible to do so as South Africa destabilises all southern Africa. Above all, the price of prevarication is proving unacceptably high and costly in human life.

Black nationalism in South Africa has learnt many lessons in its long and painful history. The difference between what is good for South African blacks and 'what is good for General Motors' has not required ANC teachers to impress itself on many. The tokenism, prestige projects and public rhetoric of the 1970s served only the image-making of Western governments and the international business community. The underlying reality of growing investment and covert military co-operation with the South African government is what impresses the black nationalists of the 1980s who will ultimately come to power. And they have made this very plain to anyone who bothers to ask.

The international corporate community do perhaps cynically believe that it will be 'business as usual' after black majority rule, and that their undeniable economic power will be the last word in deliberations about social justice and economic change. But there is no adequate historical justification for such a belief. At the 1985 Lusaka meeting it was the ANC, not the businessmen, who set out their plans for a future South Africa that involved fundamental changes. The future of South African black nationalism in the 1980s suggests a determination to gain power and transform socio-economic relations in the Republic, and the capacity ultimately to do so. Whether this transformation takes place in a totalitarian state after massive bloodshed and the destruction of the region's economy in a war lasting decades depends in some measure on the West's capacity to perceive its strategic interests in the perspective of something more than short-term company profits. For the magnitude of the change likely to take place in South Africa should be measured against the upheaval of the Iranian revolution rather than the relatively smooth transition in Zimbabwe. And the magnitude of the West's ignorance about the true political state of black communities in South Africa has had striking parallels in both Zimbabwe and Iran during the 1970s. Given the mineral wealth of the Republic, the implications of such a change and such a misunderstanding for the Western world, and for world peace, need no underlining.

It lies within the power of the West to shorten the disruptive transition to black majority rule in South Africa and, possibly, save countless lives. To do so requires an act of political will and a prudent judgement of national interests. Effective economic sanctions imposed by the USA, Britain, West Germany, Japan and France, hold out the hope of pre-empting prolonged civil war and the devastation of the South African economy. The collapse of the Rand in 1985, after only two American banks refused to renew their loans to South Africa, demonstrated the economic power in the hands of the West. If the West now fails to wield this power effectively, substituting rhetoric for decisive action, it will remain an accomplice in what follows.

Appendices

1 Basic Statistics

Population (1984) 33 million, of which 4.8 million are classed as 'white' by the South African Government, 24.1 million 'African', 0.9 million 'Asian', and 2.8 million 'Coloured'.

Area 1 221 037 square kilometres. 14 per cent of this is allocated to blacks and 86 per cent to whites.

Religion 70 per cent Christian. Important Muslim population in parts of Western Cape and Natal.

Economy GDP 1984 97.2 million Rand, of which agriculture 4.9 million, mining 13.1 million, manufacturing 22.8 million.

Trade

Imports and exports by country

	Imports 1983 Rm	Exports 1983 Rm
US	2 467,0	1 753,8
West Germany	2 235,9	753,4
Japan	1 908,3	1 546,7
UK	1 892,9	1 324,0
France	622,7	378,7
Italy	516,4	398,9
Africa	325,7	797,0
Switzerland	288,8	1 733,8
Taiwan	251,4	192,0
Netherlands	244,0	351,5
Belgium	231,2	348,2
Australia	172,3	103,4
Brazil	164,9	17,8
Sweden	163,7	28,5
Canada	155,0	119,0
Hong Kong	152,9	236,0
Israel	72,7	157,3

South Africa's main exports are gold, diamonds, coal, iron and steel, other minerals, fruit and vegetables, cereals, and sugar.

Health
Infant mortality (1982)
Africans	80 deaths in the first year per 1000 live births
Coloureds	59
Asians	21
Whites	14

Infant mortality is worse in bantustans: 190 per 1000 births in Transkei

Malnutrition
About a third of black children under the age of 14 are underweight and stunted in growth. In bantustans such as Ciskei and poor townships such as Chatsworth in Durban, the figure rises to two-thirds or more.

No of people per hospital bed
Africans	337
Coloureds	346
Asians	505
Whites	61

Health spending per head (for all race groups) 1982/3
Natal	R 74
Cape Province	R 99
Transvaal	R 57
KwaZulu	R 19
Transkei	R 25
Venda	R 25

Education
Education spending per head 1983/4
Africans	R 234
Coloureds	R 569
Asians	R 1 088
Whites	R 1 654

These figures exclude the four 'independent' bantustans, where education spending per head ranged from R 161 to R 246.

Pupil-teacher ratio 1984
Africans	41
Coloureds	26
Asians	23
Whites	19

These figures exclude the four 'independent' bantustans, where pupil-teacher ratios in 1983 ranged from 37 to 63, in primary schools.

Illiteracy

Half of all South Africans over the age of 20 are illiterate, including 52 per cent of urban Africans and 79 per cent of rural Africans, according to the president's council.

Extent of education

About 30 per cent of South Africa's labour force have had little or no education, and 36 per cent only primary. In 1983, 23 per cent of African children leaving school had not completed the first year of primary school. The total number of Africans in school has increased from around 0.8 million in the 1950s to 5½ million in 1986, partly due to rising population and partly to government policy especially after the student protests of 1976. Between 1979 and 1984, education spending rose 18.3 per cent a year in money terms, compared with inflation at 13.5 per cent.

Income distribution: According to the commercial firm Market Research Africa, average monthly household incomes in 1984 were:

Africans	R 273
Coloureds	R 624
Asians	R 1 072
Whites	R 1 834

2 Nelson Mandela: I am not prepared to sell the birthright of the people to be free

The full text of Nelson Mandela's response to the conditional offer of freedom made by P.W. Botha as read on his behalf by his daughter, Zinzi, in Jabulani, Soweto, on February 10th, 1985.

On Friday my mother and our attorney saw my father at Pollsmoor Prison to obtain his answer to Botha's offer of conditional release. The prison authorities attempted to stop this statement being made but he would have none of this and made it clear that he would make the statement to you, the people.

Strangers like Bethell from England and Professor Dash from the United States have in recent weeks been authorised by Pretoria to see my father without restriction, yet Pretoria cannot allow you, the people, to hear what he has to say directly. He should be here himself to tell you what he thinks of this statement by Botha. He is not allowed to do so. My mother, who also heard his words, is also not allowed to speak to you today.

My father and his comrades at Pollsmoor Prison send their greetings to you, the freedom-loving people of this our tragic land, in the full confidence that you will carry on the struggle for freedom. He and his comrades at Pollsmoor Prison send their very warmest greetings to Bishop Desmond Tutu. Bishop Tutu has made it clear to the world that the Nobel Peace Prize belongs to you who are the people. We salute him.

My father and his comrades at Pollsmoor Prison are grateful to the United Democratic Front, who without hesitation made this venue available to them so that they could speak to you today. My father and his comrades wish to make this statement to you, the people, first. They are clear that they are accountable to you and to you alone. And that you should hear their views directly and not through others. My father speaks not only for himself and for his comrades at Pollsmoor Prison, but he hopes he also speaks for all those in jail for their opposition to apartheid, for all those who are banished, for all those who are in exile, for all those who suffer under apartheid, for all those who are opponents of apartheid and for all those who are oppressed and exploited.

Throughout our struggle there have been puppets who have claimed to speak for you. They have made this claim, both here and abroad. They are of no consequence. My father and his colleagues will not be like them. My father says:

I am a member of the African National Congress. I have always been a member of the African National Congress and I will remain a member of the African National Congress until the day I die. Oliver Tambo is much more than a brother to me. He is my greatest friend and comrade for nearly 50 years. If there is any one amongst you who cherishes my freedom, Oliver Tambo cherishes it more, and I know that he would give his life to see me free. There is no difference between his views and mine.

I am surprised at the conditions that the government wants to impose on me. I am not a violent man. My colleagues and I wrote in 1952 to Malan asking for a round table conference to find a solution to the problems of our country, but that was ignored. When Strijdom was in power, we made the same offer. Again it was ignored. When Verwoerd was in power we asked for a national convention for all the people in South Africa to decide on their future. This, too, was in vain.

It was only then, when all other forms of resistance were no longer open to us, that we turned to armed struggle. Let Botha show that he is different to Malan, Strijdom and Verwoerd. Let him renounce violence. Let him say that he will dismantle apartheid. Let him unban the people's organisation, the African National Congress. Let him free all who have been imprisoned, banished or exiled for their opposition to apartheid. Let him guarantee free political activity so that people may decide who will govern them.

I cherish my own freedom dearly, but I care even more for your freedom. Too many have died since I went to prison. Too many have suffered for the love of freedom. I owe it to their widows, to their orphans, to their mothers and to their fathers who have grieved and wept for them. Not only I have suffered during these long, lonely, wasted years. I am not less life-loving than you are. But I cannot sell my birthright, nor am I prepared to sell the birthright of the people to be free. I am in prison as the representative of the people and of your organisation, the African National Congress, which was banned.

What freedom am I being offered while the organisation of the people remains banned? What freedom am I being offered when I may be arrested on a pass offence? What freedom am I being offered to live my life as a family with my dear wife, who remains in banishment in Brandfort? What freedom am I being offered when I must ask for permission to live in an urban area? What freedom am I being offered when I need a stamp in my pass to seek work? What freedom am I being offered when my very South African citizenship is not respected?

Only free men can negotiate. Prisoners cannot enter into contracts. Herman Toivo ja Toivo, when freed, never gave any undertaking, nor was he called upon to do so.

I cannot and will not give any undertaking at a time when I and you, the people, are not free.

Your freedom and mine cannot be separated. I will return.

3 The KAIROS Document: A Summary

Origin of the Document

The KAIROS document is a Christian, biblical and theological comment on the political crisis in South Africa today. It is an attempt by concerned Christians in South Africa to reflect on the situation of death in our country. It is a critique of the current theological models that determine the type of activities the Church engages in to try to resolve the problems of the country. It is an attempt to develop, out of this perplexing situation, an alternative biblical and theological model that will in turn lead to forms of activity that will make a real difference to the future of our country.

The document has been produced in an unique way, different from the usual traditional ways of producing such a document. It came out of a group of Christians who met to reflect on the crisis in the country and on the role of Christians in this crisis. Every participant was asked to write on a specific theme discussed in the meeting.

The second meeting critiqued the material and further assigned people to re-write and research the material. In the third discussion it was decided to make the draft available to as many Christians and Church leaders as possible throughout the country for comment and commitment.

On the 13 September 1985, when the document was submitted for publication, there were still comments and recommendations flowing in. The first publication therefore must be taken as a beginning, a basis for further discussion by all Christians in the country. Further editions will be published later.

Challenge to the Church

The political crisis in South Africa today is the KAIROS or moment of truth not only for apartheid but also for the Church. A KAIROS is a critical and decisive moment, a time of grace and opportunity, a challenge to decision and action.

What this moment of truth shows up first of all is that we are a divided Church. Some would even say there are two Churches — a White Church and a Black Church. Both the oppressor and the oppressed, who are in mortal conflict at the moment, claim loyalty to the same Church and the same faith and participate at the same table of the same Lord. How is that possible?

In relation to our political crisis there are three different theologies or ways of understanding Christian faith.

'State Theology'

The apartheid State misuses biblical texts and Christian beliefs to justify its oppression of the people. This we call 'State Theology'.

1. The State appeals to *Romans 13: 1-7* where Paul says that we should obey the State. That would be true in normal circumstances but Paul does not tell us in this text what we should do when the State becomes unjust, oppressive and tyrannical. When this happens we must say with Peter that we shall 'obey God rather than men' (Acts 5: 29). We should also read Revelations 13 where the State is described as a diabolical beast.

2. When we oppose the State and resist its oppression, the State makes use of the idea of *law and order* to try to make us feel guilty

and sinful. But 'law' here is the unjust and discriminatory laws of apartheid and 'order' here is the disorder of oppression and exploitation.

We must as Christians resist this type of 'law' and 'order' and obey the law and order of God.

3. In 'State Theology' the symbol of all evil is *communism*. Everyone who disobeys and opposes the State is called a godless, atheistic communist. And the State's idea of hell-on-earth would be a future communist take-over. They use this in an attempt to frighten people.

4. And finally the *god that the State preaches* to us is not the God of the Bible. It is an idol. It is the god of the gun, the god of oppression. In fact this god is the devil in disguise — the antichrist.

We must reject this heretical theology and its false prophets, who can even be found among the ranks of those who profess to be ministers of God's Word.

'Church Theology'

Many Church leaders who make statements and pronouncements about apartheid appeal to certain abstract Christian ideas like reconciliation, peace, justice and non-violence. This we call 'Church Theology' and we offer here our critique of this theology too. It is inadequate, irrelevant and ineffective.

1. *Reconciliation:* There can be no true reconciliation and no genuine peace without justice just as there can be no forgiveness until there is repentance. If we call for reconciliation and negotiations now, before repentance and justice and equality have been established, we will be calling for reconciliation between good and evil, justice and injustice, God and the devil. We must not come to terms with evil, we must do away with it.

2. *Justice:* True justice cannot come from the 'top', from the oppressor, in the form of concessions and reforms. Why then do Church leaders so often address their appeals to the 'top', to the State and to the White community? They (the top) must indeed repent but true justice will be determined by all the people together — as equals. Should the Church not address its appeals to the oppressed, encouraging them to take up their own cause and to struggle for justice?

3. *Non-violence:* Violence is a loaded word. What a person calls 'violence', and what they call a 'legitimate use of physical force in self-defence', depends upon which side the person is on. When Church statements call all physical force 'violence' no matter which side does it, they are trying to be neutral and to avoid saying who is right and who is wrong, who is the aggressor and who is the defendant. Of course that does not mean that every or any use of physical force by the oppressed is justifiable but it cannot be

70

condemned for the same reason and in the same way as the violence of the aggressor.

4. *The Fundamental Problem* with this kind of 'Church Theology' is that it is still influenced by a type of spirituality that tends to be other-worldly. It is only recently that the Church has come to face the realities of this world and it has not yet developed an adequate analysis of our society and an appreciation of the need for politics and political strategies. A new biblical and prophetic spirituality is needed today.

Towards a Prophetic Theology

What we need now is a prophetic theology that takes a clear and unambiguous stand in the present crisis. This will have to be based upon a reading of the signs of our times, that is to say, a *social analysis* of the conflicting forces or interests that make up our situation of oppression.

Then we will have to go back to *the Bible* to find out what God has to say about oppression and what it means to say that God is always on the side of the oppressed. In the Christian tradition we will find this same theme expounded in terms of *tyranny*. A tyrannical regime is one that has become the enemy of the common good because it governs in the interests of some of the people and not in the interests of all the people — the common good. The apartheid regime is clearly a tyrannical regime. It is therefore a *morally illegitimate* regime and should be replaced by a government that will govern in the interests of all the people.

A prophetic theology, however, will not only point out what is wrong and sinful in our society, it will also present both the oppressor and the oppressed with a relevant and explicit *message of hope*. There is hope because God has promised us in Jesus Christ that justice and truth and love will triumph over all injustice and oppression in the end.

Challenge to Action

God Sides with the Oppressed: We are a divided Church and there is only one way forward to unity and that is for those Christians who find themselves on the side of the oppressor or sitting on the fence to cross over to the other side to be united in faith and action with those who are oppressed. We must be united in Jesus Christ and in God 'who is always on the side of the oppressed' (Ps 103: 6).

Participation in the Struggle: The present crisis challenges the Church to move beyond an 'ambulance' ministry to a ministry of participation in the struggle for liberation by supporting and encouraging the campaigns and actions of the people.

Transforming Church Activities: The usual activities of the Church like Sunday services, baptisms, funerals and so forth must all be reshaped to promote the liberating mission of God in our present crisis. The evil forces we speak of in baptism, for example, must be named. We know what these evil forces are in South Africa today.

Special Campaigns: The Church should also make its contribution to the struggle by having special programmes, projects and campaigns. However, this should be done in consultation with the political organisations that truly represent the grievances and demands of the people. Otherwise there will be a serious lack of co-ordination and co-operation.

Civil Disobedience: The Church must not collaborate with tyranny and oppression. It should encourage all its members to pray and to work for a change of government. In the process the Church may sometimes have to confront the apartheid regime and even advocate civil disobedience.

Moral Guidance: It is also the role of the Church in the present crisis to provide moral guidance by helping the people to understand their rights and their duties, especially the moral duty to resist tyranny and to struggle for a just society. While it is necessary to curb the excesses of those who act wildly and thoughtlessly, the Church should be experienced as the community that challenges, inspires and motivates people.

It is hoped that this document will become the basis of discussion, reflection and action and that it will be further developed and improved by those who can hear what the Spirit has to say to the Churches in our day.

The Kairos Theologians
Braamfontein
South Africa

4 South African Council of Churches National Conference 1985 Resolution No.5: Disinvestment

The National Conference of the South African Council of Churches, being deeply concerned at the violent conflict in which the people of South Africa are now embroiled:

1 reiterates the statement which the Council has made in the past that foreign investment and loans have been used to support prevailing patterns of power and privilege in South Africa;
2 recognises that many church leaders and Christian people in South Africa are in favour of (selective) disinvestment and economic sanctions because they believe that the situation is now so serious that economic action must be taken to strengthen political and diplomatic pressures on South Africa to force the South African government to take seriously the need for fundamental change in South Africa;
3 is agreed that fundamental change would include the dismantling of apartheid and the democratic involvement of all South Africans in the planning of new political, economic and social structures which would seek to guarantee for all people justice, development, freedom and peace;
4 welcomes the concern and support of our fellow Christians in other countries who are working to assist us in finding non-violent ways in which fundamental change can be brought about in South Africa;
5 believes that the pressure in Western countries for disinvestment and divestment has been most effective in moving white South Africans into a more serious consideration of the cause of the political conflict of this country;
6 concludes from the evidence placed before it that foreign investment does not necessarily create new jobs and that the contrary is often the case because new investment is frequently in the form of sophisticated technological equipment;
7 draws attention to the fact that the churches have for many years tried to address the problem of structural unemployment in black communities and have not been aware of any serious concern being shown by the business sector, foreign or South African, or by government until recent months, when economic sanctions have become a legislative probability in the United States;
8 confesses that in the churches there has been no proper debate and consideration of the disinvestment question because we have allowed ourselves to be restrained by the severity of laws designed to prevent open discussion of economic sanctions. This has meant that the only arguments being heard in South Africa are those in opposition to disinvestment.

This Conference therefore resolves:

A to express our belief that disinvestment and similar economic pressures are now called for as a peaceful and effective means of putting pressure on the South African government to bring about those fundamental changes this country needs;
B to ask our partner churches in other countries to continue with

their efforts to identify and promote effective economic pressures to influence the situation in South Africa, towards achieving justice and peace in this country and minimising the violence of the conflict;

C to promote fuller consideration of the issues by placing the case for the imposition of economic sanctions and disinvestment before the Executive Committee of the SACC and the regional councils, and the councils of our member churches and organisations with the request that they encourage congregations to study and debate them;

D to ask the Executive to appoint in consultation with the Director of Justice and Reconciliation a task force to examine the whole question of economic justice as well as issues of disinvestment and economic sanctions, to review and co-ordinate the responses from the churches, and to assist the church leaders by making available to them information and analyses;

E to call member churches and individual Christians to withdraw from participation in the economic system that oppresses the poor, by re-investing money and energy in alternative economic systems in existence in our region.

Accepted by National Conference of SACC on 28 June 1985.

5 Statement by the Southern African Catholic Bishops' Conference on Conscription, 1985

Our concern as bishops in Southern Africa is for a speedy and just solution to the problems experienced by the people of South Africa and Namibia, a solution in which all sectors of the population are called to play their part.

The situation

In our report on Namibia, issued in 1982, we drew your attention to the fact that the majority of Namibians regard the South African

Defence Force as an army of occupation which is hindering the granting of independence to that country in terms of Resolution 435 of the UN Security Council.

During the unrest in the Vaal and East Rand townships in late 1984 the army was deployed for the first time in a support capacity to the South African Police operating in those areas. This action was greeted with shock and horror by the inhabitants of those townships and by other South Africans concerned about how and where the army is deployed.

This use of the army to enforce 'law and order' within the country has been further extended in 1985 to include the townships in the Eastern Cape, despite all the protests that the legitimate use of an army is in the protection of the country's borders.

Many young men who are conscripted each year into the South African Defence Force are experiencing crises of conscience as they become aware of the role that they are being expected to play in the black townships, and elsewhere in South Africa. As far back as 1977, out of our concern about the nature of the armed struggle and the escalating violence in Southern Africa, we defended the right of every individual to follow his own conscience, the right therefore to conscientious objection both on the grounds of universal pacificism and on the grounds that a person may seriously believe the war to be unjust.

We believe that a serious decision of this nature is a moral judgement and must be made after deep and prayerful examination of the facts available. In 1977 we urged the South African government to make provision for alternative forms of non-military national service, as is found in other parts of the world. In 1983, in a letter to the Minister of Defence about the proposed Defence Amendment Act, Cardinal McCann, on our behalf, pointed out to the minister that the proposed amendments, making it possible for Christian pacifists to refuse military training, did not go far enough. Provision should also be made for so-called moral or ethical objectors. At that time we stated that if such an amendment was not included in the Defence Amendment Act we would find it necessary to reject the Act as unjust.

Our suggestion

Our suggested amendment was not included in the Defence Amendment Act. The situation in Southern Africa has continued to deteriorate and in 1985 we find ourselves in a situation of grave crisis.

We are concerned at the growing numbers of young men put into an invidious position by their conscription, with the choices of leaving the country, or facing six years' imprisonment, or six years' alternative service for refusing to join the South African Defence Force, or else of serving in an army with whose mode of operation

75

they cannot agree. We recognise that an end to conscription would leave membership of the South African Defence Force open to those who are in sympathy with it and would grant individuals freedom of conscience in determining their response to the situation. Therefore we join our voices with those who have already asked for an end to conscription. We call on the government to amend the Defence Act to make this possible. We also encourage Catholics to help promote peace by working for an end to conscription in whatever ways lie open to them.

6 United States Catholic Conference Administrative Board Statement on South Africa, September 11, 1985

The relationship between the United States and South Africa has entered a new period of tension and trouble. The determined resistance of the black population of South Africa to the whole political, legal, economic and social system of apartheid presents a moral and political challenge to the rest of the world.

The attention of the international community is now focused on South Africa because of recent instances of violent resistance to apartheid. In South Africa violence has spawned violence. The system of apartheid inflicts its own kind of violence on the human person every day.

The Catholic Bishops of South Africa characterized apartheid in 1957 as 'something intrinsically evil.' Their judgement found resounding affirmation in the address of Pope John Paul II at the Hague in March 1985:

> For Christians and for all who believe in a covenant, that is an unbreakable bond between God and man and between all human beings, no form of discrimination — in law or in fact — on the basis of race, origins, color, culture, sex or religion can ever be acceptable. Hence no system of apartheid or separate development will ever be acceptable as a model for the relations between people or races.

On August 3, 1985, after a State of Emergency was declared by the South African Government, the Catholic Bishops of that country declared:

'Hearing of the tragic events in our country, Pope John Paul II last week spoke of this apartheid policy in these words: "To those who suffer the violence of such an inhuman situation I express sentiments of profound participation and support." And we say now, as long as the system of apartheid prevails, the resentment and the unrest will never die down.

In our report on police conduct during township protests, in December 1984, and our statement of March 22 on the Langa tragedy, we deplored the unnecessary force and violence used by the police. We deplore the violence that has continued: the violence of the system. The violence of the police — acknowledging proper fulfilment of duty where this has occurred — and the violence of those who, angered and frustrated beyond measure, have pursued in reprisal and political antagonism the path of destruction, injury, intimidation and even killing.

This is the way of anarchy and chaos. The system bears the gravest responsibility for it. And unless the system is changed, the violence is not likely to abate.'

The religious and moral significance of the South African problem is evident in these statements. The central question posed by apartheid is a direct attack on the dignity of the human person. At the foundation of the Biblical vision and the Christian tradition is the conviction that every person is created in the image of God. Every person reflects the presence of God among us; apartheid tries to define the ultimate value of the person on the basis of race and color. Christian teaching demands that the unique dignity of every person should find expression in the protection and promotion of the human rights of the person; apartheid is a systematic assault on the basic rights of black and coloured races in South Africa. Christian teaching holds that the state has a positive moral responsibility toward the welfare of every person; the apartheid system places the resources of the state decisively in the service of the minority of the South African population. On item after item apartheid stands as a contradiction to the basic Christian teaching on human dignity and the human person.

It is clear on human, moral and political grounds that change must come in South Africa. It is also clear that the primary agents of change are within South Africa. But nations and institutions which have a relationship with South Africa are part of the political and moral drama being played out in that nation.

External forces can be catalysts for positive change or they can be obstacles to change. Insofar as this is true, external actors are not passive spectators of the South African problem, but participants in it. Moreover, they are not 'interfering' in an internal issue when they evaluate their policies or exert pressure on South Africa; they are simply exercising moral responsibility for their actions as nations or other social institutions. The policy choices of nations which have diplomatic relations with South Africa and the practices of institutions which affect South African society from the outside are filled with moral content. Determining how a given policy choice will influence the apartheid system is not a simple matter. But this is no excuse for avoiding choices . . .

Different parts of US society — our government, churches, corporations, foundations — have a direct influence on South Africa; they affect how the people and government of South Africa see the United States.

We speak as bishops and pastors of a Church whose religious and moral teaching is daily contradicted by apartheid, and whose brother bishops are actively opposing apartheid. We also speak as citizens of a nation which exercises a significant influence in South African society. We use this statement to express our episcopal solidarity with the Southern African Catholic Bishops' Conference and to express our deep respect for the exemplary ecumenical witness for justice being made by the churches of South Africa. The words and actions of church leaders in South Africa challenge us to address the moral choices our own society faces concerning South Africa.

I. The Church: As members of the Administrative Board of the United States Catholic Conference, we recommend the following actions:

First, that the members of the Catholic Church in the United States be informed about the basic facts of life in South Africa, including the nature of apartheid, its concomitant denial of basic human rights, and its disastrous effects upon individuals and families in the political, legal, economic, and social spheres.

Second, that the members of the Catholic Church in the United States be urged to pray for the people and churches of South Africa and Namibia, as requested by the churches of those countries.

Third, that the US Catholic Conference continue to strengthen its fraternal relationship with the Southern African Catholic Bishops' Conference through visits, communications, and collaboration.

Fourth, that the US Catholic Conference, in consultation with the Southern African Catholic Bishops' Conference, support appropriate legislation in the US Congress and communicate its views on matters of policy to members of the Executive Branch of the US government.

Fifth, that the US Catholic Conference, in consultation with the Southern African Catholic Bishops' Conference, consider ways in which assistance may be given to those South Africans who conscientiously object to service in the military forces of South Africa.

Sixth, that the USCC Committee on Social Development and World Peace continue its study of the question of divestment of church funds from business enterprises and banks doing business in South Africa and report on this subject to the Administrative Board.

II. The US Government: the United States is a major force in the diplomatic life of South Africa and this offers the possibility of effective action by the United States government to bring about fundamental change in South Africa before that country is engulfed in a full-scale civil war. As Bishop Desmond Tutu said on August 15, 1985, 'Our last hope is the intervention of the international community.' Aware of this responsibility, we recommend the following policies or actions to the US government:

First, an unambiguous US policy of commitment to human rights in South Africa. It should be clear to all interested parties that the urgency of the human rights problem there has made it the principal concern of the United States in US-South African relations.

Second, the voice and vote of the United States in multinational institutions, including the United Nations General Assembly and Security Council, should be used to help make the international community's opposition to the policy of apartheid ever more vigorous and effective.

Third, the US government should engage in the aggressive diplomatic pursuit of every reasonable action in support of the dismantling of the system of apartheid as called for by the Southern African Catholic Bishops' Conference.

Fourth, the approval of the Anti-Apartheid Action Act of 1985, now pending before the Congress, which includes the following measures:

— prohibits the importation of South African krugerrands or other gold coins from South Africa;

— prohibits the exportation of computers, software and technology to the South African police, military and other government entities that enforce restrictions on Blacks' freedom of movement;

— prohibits loans to the South African government (except for loans for any educational, housing or health facility which is available to all persons on a nondiscriminatory basis);

— prohibits the export of goods or technology to be used in any South African nuclear production or utilization facility;

— imposes mandatory fair employment practices (the Sullivan principles) for US nationals controlling companies in South Africa;

— establishes a policy calling for the imposition of economic sanctions against South Africa if significant progress has not been made within twelve months toward ending apartheid;

— provides monies for scholarships for black South Africans to attend South African universities, colleges, and secondary schools;

— provides monies for a human rights fund for the legal defense of

79

victims of apartheid. The Executive Order of September 9, 1985, addresses some of these measures and we welcome it as a development in US policy. Nevertheless the Anti-Apartheid Action Act of 1985 offers a stronger and broader approach which we still believe is necessary.

Fifth, in addition to US action directed toward the internal problems of South Africa, there should be a renewed US commitment to achieve the implementation of UN Resolution 435 in Namibia, guaranteeing the withdrawal of South Africa from Namibia, a ceasefire and the holding of elections under UN auspices.

III. The Private Sector: Non-governmental institutions based in the United States with operations in South Africa can play a very significant role in promoting a consistent policy vision toward South Africa; the private sector, particularly the business and banking communities, has unique opportunities in the South Africa situation; we recommend consideration of the following:

— investment policies are particularly sensitive and crucial issues; the intense debate surrounding the disinvestment question highlights its importance; similar debate should be encouraged concerning the question of *no further investment* in South Africa and *no further bank loans* without corresponding specific steps on political, social and legal issues at stake in South Africa. It should be made clear that investments and bank loans to South Africa carry grave moral burdens and have critical impact on issues of human rights.

— labor practices and working conditions constitute another visible forum for action by US based businesses; adherence to the Sullivan principles, support for black trade unions in South Africa and creative steps to improve the general working conditions and access to positions of responsibility for blacks are all steps we find worthy of support.

No list of specifics will capture the range of choices facing individuals and institutions in the United States concerning South Africa. We use these principles and examples to press forward the widespread public debate now engaging the US government, the Congress, the business and financial communities, the media and the US public.

Change in South Africa cannot come too quickly for those bearing the indignity and the injustice of apartheid. The United States as a nation and a society should be and should be seen by others to be unambiguously in support of profound, rapid and thorough change in the political, legal, social and economic sectors of South African society.

7 The British Churches

A. Whose Rubicon?
Report of a visit to South Africa by representatives of the British churches, September 1985 (extracts)

1. Principal Conclusions

Our visit to South Africa has convinced us that the situation has radically changed since the beginning of this year — not merely intensified, but moved into an entirely new phase. The real initiative has passed to the black population, despite its weakness, while the institutions of power, for all their massive strength, can do no more than react ever more violently to each fresh development.

Black South Africans are no longer prepared to accept 'solutions' imposed, or even proposed, by others. They feel they have waited too long for a change of heart in the white population of the Republic as a whole, or for effectual intervention by governments or businesses outside. They have learned to mistrust any dependence upon the wisdom or goodwill of others, though they remain extraordinarily open and welcoming towards any individual with courage and compassion enough to share their struggle. They still hope for a unitary, non-racial nation, and the great majority of them would prefer to achieve it by non-violent means, though they believe the use of violence is justified by their circumstances.

So any reform or constitutional change originated by the present government of South Africa would be unacceptable to the black population in general, however ameliorative or far-reaching it might be. Any consultation or any form of power-sharing in which the black participants were selected by the whites would be equally unacceptable. Any new constitution devised and proposed by intermediaries in Britain or elsewhere would be rejected no less by Blacks than by Whites. For their demand is quite simply a genuine and substantial participation through freely chosen and trusted representatives in framing a new constitution to establish a more just, democratic and unified society. It is this will to share in decision-making that is symbolized in the demand for the release of Nelson Mandela.

But it is precisely this change which the South African government and its supporters are unwilling, and perhaps unable, to contemplate. The essence of apartheid is not separate seats and entrances, nor even separate townships or separate school systems, all of which can be subject to reform, but the ingrained assumption that Blacks must remain subservient, at best to white paternalism, or at worst to white

81

tyranny. We can see no hope of stability in South Africa until those who hold power concede the right of any of the inhabitants of the Republic, of whatever colour, to organize opposition to the status quo and press for change, within the normal bounds of legitimacy in a civilized democratic state. Up to the present the evidence suggests that those who hold power are incapable of admitting that right. Whenever the legitimate non-violent dissent of Blacks, Coloureds or Indians has achieved any strength and coherence, instead of being heard it has been maligned as treasonable or communist, its organization banned, its leaders detained or eliminated, and its active following harassed with shocking brutality. It was inevitable that this repression of opposition should issue in an escalation of violence, the involvement of the armed forces and ultimately in civil war.

The tragic element in this history is the failure of a white population that see themselves as honourable, humane and freedom-loving to recognise the cruel injustice being perpetrated on their behalf and to find it intolerable. Many of them dislike the more rigorous instances of apartheid and hope for some amelioration, but few, even today, have any awareness of the pain and despair which the system inflicts. There have been prophets enough, crying in the wilderness, but for the most part the response remains the same: 'What they say cannot be true; they are repeating the lies put about by the enemies of our country.' The only answer to this is: 'Go to the townships, the resettlement areas, the advice centres for the families of detainees, and see for yourselves.' And this they find very difficult to do. One is chillingly reminded of the decent citizens of Germany in the 1930s. And it has to be said that now, as then, the churches and their clergy, with many heroic exceptions, have not been assiduous enough in opening the minds of their membership to the realities surrounding them.

In the name of reconciliation they have avoided taking sides, even when such avoidance became a betrayal of the truth. There is grave need for a Confessing Church to emerge among the white congregations in South Africa, and indeed it is already appearing there; the unanimity of the Roman Catholic Bishops and the theological challenge of the recent 'Kairos' document are signs of its coming to birth. There is no less need for a Confessing Church movement in Britain if our people are to be ready for the moral and spiritual testing which the struggle in South Africa is bringing upon us.

The immediate practical issue before our nation is whether to join others in bringing economic pressures to bear upon the South African government. Britain has a particular responsibility to decide this question aright because of the high level of her trade with, and investment in, the Republic. And, since right decisions are not made from false assumptions, we must first abandon two familiar arguments that are not supported by the facts. The policy of 'constructive engagement' has had no effect upon the crucial injustice of the situation, namely the rejection of an authentic black participation in decision-making. Secondly, the great majority of blacks, well aware of the new hardships they will suffer as a result of disinvestment, would nevertheless welcome it as a sign of commitment to their cause. If that commitment is lacking, our application of economic pressure will be an empty show, and this may explain the faintly sceptical tone in which black people responded when we sought their opinion. They would welcome an effective augmentation of their own efforts, but they are not now expecting the struggle to be resolved by forces outside South Africa. On the other hand, the extreme sensitivity of the South African government on this issue and the recent determined reactions from big business give good grounds for hoping that selective and specific economic pressure by Britain might hasten the day of radical change and reduce the period of bloody conflict. A total application of sanctions has elsewhere proved to be too blunt and faulty an instrument to achieve a calculated result. But a ban on all new investment, selective disinvestment, especially in the field of high technology, a boycott of South African exports and, above all, a withdrawal of loan facilities by banks, following the example of Chase Manhattan, might achieve notable results if applied with the declared end of bringing the government of the Republic to negotiate a radically new constitution with the authentic leadership of the various population groups.

A more far-reaching change of attitude is urgently required, however, of the people of Britain which goes beyond the tactics we may employ, and may need to precede them. For forty years or more voices have been raised in South Africa pleading for more decisive intervention to end oppression. We have lived in the belief that, while time was perhaps running out, someone, if not ourselves, would act to avert disaster. But the clock does not forever stand at five minutes to midnight. The crisis that has overtaken South Africa in this year signals the beginning of a day of judgement. It is not merely that pent-up forces have started to boil over; the terms of the confrontation are quite different. One might say that those who have for so long asked to be heard have now withdrawn from communication and committed themselves to action and suffering.

It is a change that needs to be understood theologically. Familiarity with the Bible throws up a number of frightening images — the last of Moses' many attempts to move the heart of Pharaoh: 'I will see thy face again no more' — Jesus' silence before Pilate. It has all been said. The case stands. Events take over from decisions already made. There are no more choices, but the secrets of all hearts are revealed through the inescapable question: Whose side are you on? That is the 'trial by ordeal' to which we ask in the Lord's Prayer that we may never come. But come we must, once in a while, just as Jesus had to. As individuals, and even more, perhaps, as nations, we are brought to test — 'If thou hadst known in this day, even thou, the things which belong unto peace.' As conflict intensifies in South Africa and violence escalates, shall this nation remember that an oppressed people, who sought for many decades to forego violence, is resisting tyranny, or shall we line up in the last resort with those of our own colour and culture? Will British bankers and businessmen continue, as some have now begun, to throw their weight on the side of equity for the sake of stability, or, as they learn that the traditional values of all black Africans tend towards a corporate economy akin to socialism, will their fight be only to preserve western capitalism?

We have seen, therefore, that, in regard to the crisis in South Africa, the most urgent responsibility of the Churches in Britain is to educate their own constituencies so as to bring about that changed understanding, that 'repentance', which is needed to make them ready for the moral and spiritual testing which the struggle in South Africa is bringing upon our nation. As part of this educative process we must be prepared to use the catalyst of a campaign for more effective economic pressure upon the South African government and more substantial support of the agencies of liberation in that land. But in that case it will be even more important to enhance the awareness and responsible action of church members towards the victims of poverty, racial tension and escalating violence in our own cities.

. . . In what follows we offer some detailed recommendations about what this might entail.

(1) Commitment:

We must work out in many areas of our life what it means to be committed to the justice of the cause of the oppressed black majority in South Africa. This will entail entering into the 'psychic anguish' of black South Africans and as Christians regularly holding our sisters and brothers in their suffering, before God in prayer and meditation. It will require repentance on our part, realistic and informed intercession and costly action.

(2) The Churches and the British Government:

We do not believe that the British Prime Minister is well-informed about what is happening in South Africa. The position of the British government, as explained by representatives of the Foreign Office, both in London and Pretoria, reflects much too clearly the views of the English-speaking business community with whom British business has close ties based on self-interest. But, while the members of the group play an important role in the economy of South Africa, politically they constitute a small minority whose motives are distrusted by urban blacks. The British government does not understand what is happening in South Africa because it is not in touch with those who know. For our government to be so committed to British commercial interests and the interests of a minority of white South Africans when wider issues of justice and righteousness are so clamant is a shame not to be tolerated by British Christians. We believe therefore that the Churches should call upon the British government both to widen its contacts within South Africa and with South Africans in exile to bring increased pressure to bear upon the South African government.

Some ways in which this might be done are:

— by applying fully EEC and Commonwealth sanctions;
— by exerting additional economic pressure through carefully targeted sanctions;
— by continuing to call for the release of Nelson Mandela;
— by continuing to make representations in the strongest possible terms to the South African government regarding the action of the SADF and the SAP in the townships and the assaults on and the torture of detainees;
— by arranging meetings at Ministerial level with ANC leaders;
— by sending observers to the treason trials in South Africa;
— by allocating funds to the oppressed in South Africa through channels acceptable to them;
— by making it possible for more black South Africans to receive scholarships for further training in South Africa and overseas.

(3) Information

Since the delegation returned to Britain the South African government has placed a ban on news-stories about what is happening in black urban areas covered by the State of Emergency. The intention is that only the government's view of the conflict be heard both by its own people and by concerned observers abroad. Mass non-violent protest requires an audience to be effective, and the South African government is seeking to deny black people access to their audience. In a situation such as this the information and education departments of our churches have a special role to play in communicating what is happening, how events are perceived by the oppressed majority and how we as Christians interpret what is taking place. Churches should challenge their departments to increase their efforts and make more skilled resources available.

(4) Partner Churches in South Africa

In the light of our commitment to the oppressed, how should we relate to our traditional partner-churches? If a Confessing Church begins to emerge, how does this challenge our traditional links? The delegation believes the move to a Confessing Church must be welcomed, but the implications are profound.

(5) Visits and Personal Contacts:

Is every contact and visit right and proper?

Can we still visit South Africa and talk with all parties? And if so on what conditions? Whom should we receive in Britain? If only some contacts are admissible what is the theology of this? The delegation asks that attention be given to these questions and recommends that

— more opportunities be provided for representatives of the struggle to visit Britain, to be received by the churches and to speak of their experience.

— more scholarship funds be made available to enable black leaders of all kinds to pursue training in South Africa, and if necessary, in the United Kingdom.

(6) Financial Commitment of the Churches:

Is what we do adequate? If not what more must be done?

(a) to provide help to the poor in South Africa.

(b) to help those who have suffered in the struggle within South Africa by providing funds for bail, for legal costs, for the support of dependants of detainees and political prisoners and for community work.

(c) to aid those of all races who have chosen exile and in particular the members of the Liberation Movement and those who have refused conscription.

(d) to maintain the expertises of the British Churches in this field:

Political expertise: Division of International Affairs of the BCC; Catholic Institute for International Relations.

Economic expertise: Christian Concern for Southern Africa.

Grant-making expertise: Christian Aid and The Catholic Fund for Overseas Development.

Expertise in the spreading of information.

Theological expertise.

The education of our British constituency.

Links with the Trade Union Movement.

Should any funds we give to sister Churches in South Africa be reviewed in the light of new commitments?

(7) The Investment Policies of the British Churches:

There is a continuing pressing obligation upon the British Churches to scrutinise the practices of our financial institutions to ensure that as institutions we are not profiting from the oppression we condemn.

86

We commend the work of the Ethical Investment Research and Information Service (EIRIS) and Christian Concern for Southern Africa (CCSA) and call upon Churches to provide funds to develop their expertise and to use their resources to make our investment policies more just.

(8) Sanctions:

Careful work, drawing upon political, economic and theological expertise, needs to be continued on how to implement the clear call that came to the delegation from the majority of the black population for economic pressure to be exerted upon the regime. We are glad that resolutions before the Assembly of the BCC in November 1985 bring detailed proposals about targeted sanctions.

(9) Church and State:

The South African experience challenges the British Churches to re-think how certain key theological categories can be applied in the political arena. The KAIROS document demands a response, especially with regard to reconciliation, tyrannicide and violent revolution.

(10) The Economic Future of South Africa:

South Africans face certain crucial questions about the future and while they are arriving at their own conclusions, we too are challenged to declare our position. For example:

(a) How is the present situation to be analysed? How have white racism and economic oppression interacted to create the present conflict and has one of these been more dominant than the other? What is the consequence of this analysis for the future? Is there a Christian view?

(b) Two main types of society are on offer as models for the South Africa of the future — the capitalist, free enterprise model and the socialist model. The British business community has a considerable vested interest in influencing the choice that will be made. British Churches have a great responsibility to be informed at an expert level about these issues and to share in common action.

(c) Studies of poverty in South Africa suggest that no economic system yet devised on the African continent can alleviate the distress of the poor to the point of satisfying the aspirations now being expressed by blacks. In fact it seems to be inevitable that their lot will get very much worse. Christians have a special concern for the poor: what is to be the response of the British Churches?

The members of the delegation believe that these are important questions both for South Africa and for British Christianity. We commend them to the churches.

B. British Council of Churches resolution, November 1985

1. The Assembly:

convinced that it is immoral to profit from investment in the gravely unjust system of apartheid, a system falsely claiming to safeguard Christian values, and

conscious that a radical transformation of society is longed for by those on whom the indignity, injustice and violence of apartheid are inflicted, and

aware that the policy of 'constructive engagement' has not contributed to the participation of black South Africans in the government of their country:

reaffirms the BCC's policy (November 1979) that 'progressive disengagement from the economy of South Africa is the appropriate basic approach for churches to adopt until all the people share equally in the exercise of political power';

requests member churches to urge their financial authorities to cease, where they have not already done so, to invest in companies which have a substantial stake in the South African economy; and

calls on all Christian people to identify personally with the peaceful struggle against apartheid by refusing to buy or sell South African products.

2. The Assembly

i. *commends* the report prepared by the British Churches' delegation to South Africa;

ii. *gives thanks* that an increasing number of church people in South Africa are working for justice; and

iii. *urges* Christians to pray for all the people of South Africa and for a more just political order;

iv. *accepts* that the report's analysis of the racial and political situation in South Africa demands that all the people should participate in decisions about their future through their own acknowledged leaders;

v. *noting* the June 1985 resolution of the SACC which expresses the belief that 'disinvestment and similar economic sanctions are now called for as a peaceful and effective means of putting pressure on the South African government to bring about the fundamental changes this country needs;

vi. *resolves that,* given the deepening crisis in South Africa and the Christian duty to promote its just resolution, BCC policy will be strong advocacy of and full support for carefully targeted sanctions;

vii *calls on* the Executive Committee and the member Churches of the Council to maintain active dialogue with HMG in pursuance of the common objective of promoting the end of apartheid.

7 World Council of Churches: Harare Declaration

We, leaders of churches from Western Europe, North America, Australia, South Africa and other parts of Africa, along with representatives of WCC (World Council of Churches), WARC (World Alliance of Reformed Churches), LWF (Lutheran World Federation) and AACC (All Africa Conference of Churches) met here in Harare, Zimbabwe, from the 4th to the 6th of December 1985 on the invitation of the World Council of Churches.

We have come together to seek God's guidance at this time of profound crisis in South Africa, and have committed ourselves to a continuing theological reflection on the will of God for the church. We affirm that the moment of truth (KAIROS) is now, both for South Africa and the world community. We have heard the cries of anguish of the people of South Africa trapped in the oppressive structures of apartheid. In this moment, of immense potentiality, we agree that the apartheid structure is against God's will, and is morally indefensible. The government has no credibility. We call for an end to the State of Emergency, the release of Nelson Mandela and all political prisoners, the lifting of the state of emergency, the unbanning of all banned movements, and the return of exiles. The transferring of power to the majority of the people, based on universal suffrage, is the only lasting solution to the present crisis.

We understand and fully support those in South Africa who are calling for the resignation of the government. We regard this as the most appropriate and least costly process of change and as a contribution towards such a change. As we await a new democratic and representative government in South Africa, then:

1. We call on the Church inside and outside South Africa to continue praying for the people of South Africa and to observe June 16th — the tenth anniversary of the Soweto uprising — as World Day of Prayer and Fast to end unjust rule in South Africa.
2. We call on the international community to prevent the extension, rolling over, or renewal of bank loans to the South African government, banks, corporations and para-state institutions.
3. We call on the international community to apply immediate and comprehensive sanctions on South Africa.
4. We call on the Church inside and outside South Africa to support South African movements working for the liberation of their country.

5. We welcome and support the recent developments within the Trade Union movement for a united front against apartheid.
6. We demand the immediate implementation of the United Nations Resolution 435 on Namibia.

We, gathered here, commit ourselves to the implementation of the Harare Declaration as a matter of urgency. We are confident that the liberation of South Africa will be liberation for all the people in the country, black and white.

Harare, Zimbabwe
December 6, 1985

Select Index of Persons and Organisations